CONTENTS

PREFACE

This Arabic Phrase Book has the same excellent pedigree as all others in the Hugo series, having been compiled by experts to meet the general needs of tourists and business travellers, but it is – as you might expect – slightly different. Arranged under the usual headings of 'Hotels', 'Motoring' and so forth, the Arabic words and phrases you may need to use are printed in familiar roman letters, following an easy-to-use imitated pronunciation system that is fully explained on page 5. You should have no difficulty reading these phrases, but if you use our audio cassette of selected extracts from the book, then you should be word-perfect! Ask your bookseller for the Hugo Arabic Travel Pack.

Of course you will want to know what various signs and notices mean when they are written in Arabic; there are lists of common signs (pages 18-19) and road signs (pages 26-29), as well as recognition boxes headed *Things you'll see* in most sections of the book. These cover words, signs, notices etc; the Arabic script is given alongside its romanized pronunciation and the English translation.

Also included is a special section covering business talk. There is a 2000-line mini-dictionary to help you form additional phrases (or at least express the one word you need!), and the extensive menu reader will ease your way through some 300 Arabic dishes, basic foods, drinks and methods of cooking. Guidance on aspects of the Arabic way of life – points of etiquette, good manners and customs – will be found under the heading *Cross-cultural Notes;* an understanding of such matters will greatly enhance your trip, and your hosts will appreciate the effort you have made to respect their culture and to speak their language.

PRONUNCIATION

When reading the imitated pronunciation, stress that part of the word which is underlined. Pronounce each word as if it were an English word and you will be understood sufficiently well.

a, -ah	as in 'mad'
aa	as in 'far'
aw	as in 'law'
ay	as in 'day'
e	as in 'bed'
ee	as in 'sheen'
i	as in 'bit'
o	as in 'rob'
oo	as in 'food'
u	as in 'book'

A	pronounced like a heavy, forced 'a', as in 'both of us – you And me!'
D	a heavily pronounced 'd'
gh	like a French 'r' – from the back of the throat
H	a heavily pronounced 'h'
kh	as in the Scottish pronunciation of 'loch'
q	a 'k' sound from the back of the mouth – as in 'caramel'
S, T	heavily pronounced 's, t'
th	as in 'thin'
Z	a heavily pronounced 'z'
'	this sounds like a small catch in the breath

When two vowels occur together each is pronounced separately. So for example in 'Ae-' and 'aA' each of the vowels are pronounced separately.

Note also that 'e' always has the same value – so, for example, in the Arabic 'be-' the 'e' is pronounced as in the word 'bed'.

5

CROSS-CULTURAL NOTES

The Arab world comprises some nineteen different states covering a vast geographical area. Manners and customs vary greatly depending upon each country's history, geography and climate, local conditions and the general level of development and national wealth. Nevertheless, there are several general cross-cultural differences which apply to all Arab countries to a greater or lesser degree and which should be borne in mind by all travellers to the Arab world whether they go there for business reasons or for pleasure.

Handshaking, and occasionally embracing, is the Arab greeting. If you are introduced to a group of Arabs you should shake them all by the hand in turn, starting with the most senior and ending with the youngest. When you address your Arab colleagues in business you should normally use their first name ie Muhammad, Ali, Hussein etc and prefix it by 'ya sayed...' (Mr ...). On the very rare occasions that you meet ladies in business you use 'ya sayedah' instead. If the person you are addressing is particularly eminent or has some rank, you can substitute 'ya ostaaz ...' (sir ...). You will normally be addressed by your first name prefixed in the same way, ie 'ya sayed John' and so on. In less formal contexts you will find people just use the first name prefixed by 'ya ...'.

Most socialising you do with Arabs will probably take place in the context of an hotel, restaurant or café. The rules of behaviour are just the same as they are in the West, although you will find that most Arabs have not acquired the habits of swearing, drinking and gaming that are so common elsewhere.

If you are invited into an Arab's home, however, you will find that in all probability traditional Arab customs and assumptions still hold sway. The most notable cultural difference is the partial or total segregation of women from all men but their husband and close family relations. As a male Western visitor you may not see a single woman during your visit – although this is changing in many large cities and in the more cosmopolitan countries such as Egypt.

You will probably find that a meal has been timed to coincide with your visit. This will often come in the form of a large dish or dishes of food being laid on a cloth on the floor or low table. The guests then either sit on cushions on the floor or on low seats and help themselves to food with a spoon or fork, without plates. Usually flat bread is served which can be used to coax awkward morsels onto the spoon or fork! The meal will end with very small cups of bitter, strong black coffee or sweet tea served from a samovar. It is usual to take two or three cups and when you have had enough you just shake your cup before returning it to your host.

In large hotels you will certainly find Western-style toilets to sit on but everywhere else you will only find the 'Turkish' variety. This is a porcelain base with foot supports and a hole. Although these are not comfortable or easy to use there is no reason why they should be less hygienic than the Western variety. You are strongly advised to carry a good supply of toilet paper or tissues with you at all times.

It is considered ill-mannered to use your left hand to shake hands or to eat with as it is thought of as the 'unclean' hand.

You will find that Arabs dress more smartly than many Westerners, especially young Arabs, and you should try and look smart too and avoid wearing shorts or anything particularly skimpy.

There is no getting away from the fact that women are not considered to have equal status with men in Arab society, although this is gradually changing. Conditions for women vary greatly, although nowhere is it a good idea for a woman to travel alone. In the pavement cafés of Cairo it is quite acceptable for a woman to sip a beer. But in Saudi Arabia a woman may not even drive a car, let alone sit in a public place drinking anything.

For the alcohol-loving traveller the Arab world is definitely not the place. Alcohol is available in Egypt, Jordan and some other countries but it is absolutely forbidden in Saudi Arabia and most of the other states of the peninsula. Your trip to the Arab world is the ideal time to give your liver a holiday as well, since fruit juices are cheap, plentiful and fresh.

USEFUL EVERDAY PHRASES

Yes/no
naAm/laa

Thank you
shokran

No, thank you
laa shokran

Please *(offering)*
tafaDal

Please *(asking for something)*
min faDlak

I don't understand
ma afham

Do you speak English/French/German?
hal tatakalam engleezee/faransee/almaanee?

I can't speak Arabic
ma aqdar atakalam Arabee

I don't know
ma aAref

Please speak more slowly
law samaHt takalam sheway sheway

Please write it down for me
law samaHt ektobha Ala hazah al-waraqah

My name is ...
esmee ...

How do you do, pleased to meet you
kayf Haalak, tasharafna be-meArefatak

Good morning
SabaaH al-khayr

Good afternoon
as-salaam Alaykum

Good evening
masa' al-khayr

Good night *(when going to bed)*
tesbaH Ala khayr

Good night *(leaving group early)*
maA as-salaamah *or* as-salaam Alaykum

Goodbye
maA as-salaamah

How are you?
kayf Haalak

Excuse me please
min faDlak, law samaHt

Sorry!
aasef

I'm really sorry
aasef jeddan

USEFUL EVERYDAY PHRASES

Can you help me?
min faDlak, momken tosaAednee?

Can you tell me?
min faDlak, momken taqool lee ...?

Can I have ...?
min faDlak, momken aakhoz ..?

I would like ...
oreed ...

Is there ... here?
fee .. hona?

Where can I get ...?
min wayn ajeeb ...?

How much is it?
bekam?

What time is it?
as-saAh kam?

I must go now
laazem arooH fawran

I've lost my way
ana Dalayt aT-Tareeq

Cheers!
fee SeHatak!

Do you take credit cards?
hal taqbal Visa, Access?

10

Where is the toilet?
wayn at-towaal<u>ee</u>t?

Go away!
<u>e</u>mshee!

Excellent!
momt<u>aa</u>z

THINGS YOU'LL HEAR

<u>A</u>fwan?	Pardon?
<u>a</u>l-Hamdo lellah, sh<u>o</u>kran – wa <u>a</u>nta?	Very well thank you – and you?
be-ash<u>oo</u>fak baAd<u>ay</u>n	See you later
bej<u>a</u>dd?	Is that so?
ensh<u>aa</u>llah	God (Allah) willing
kayf H<u>aa</u>lak?	How are you?
kayf H<u>aa</u>lak, tash<u>a</u>rafna be-moq<u>aa</u>belatak	How do you do, nice to meet you
kh<u>a</u>lee b<u>aa</u>lak!	Look out!
maA as-sal<u>aa</u>mah	Goodbye
ma <u>a</u>fham	I don't understand
ma <u>a</u>Aref	I don't know
m<u>aa</u>lesh!	What does it matter!
SaH<u>ee</u>H	That's right
sh<u>o</u>kran	Thanks
taf<u>a</u>Dal	Here you are
tash<u>a</u>rafna	You're welcome
ya mo<u>A</u>lem!	Hey!

11

THINGS YOU'LL SEE

الدخول مجاناً	**ad-dokhool majaanan**	admission free
مغلق	**moghlaq**	closed
مغلق للعطلة	**moghlaq lil-AoTlah**	closed for holiday period
تفضل للداخل	**tafaDDal lid-daakhil**	come straight in
ماء للشرب	**ma' lil-shorb**	drinking water
مخرج الطوارىء	**makhraj aT-Tawaare'**	emergency exit
مصعد	**meSAd**	lift
مسجد	**masjed**	mosque
ممنوع الدخول	**mamnooA ad-dokhool**	no admittance
مدينة قديمة	**madeenah qadeemah**	old city
مفتوح	**maftooH**	open
مشغول	**mashghool**	engaged
شقة للايجار	**shaqqah lil-eejaar**	flat for rent
ممنوع	**mamnooA**	forbidden
للبيع	**lil-bayA**	for sale
رجال	**rejaal**	gentlemen
سيدات	**sayedaat**	ladies →

مواعيد العمل	**mawaAeed al-Amal**	opening times
خاص	**khaaS**	private
اسحب	**esHab**	pull
ادفع	**edfaA**	push
محجوز	**maHjooz**	reserved
آثار	**aathaar**	ruins
أوكازيون	**ookaazyoon**	sale
مبيعات	**mabeeAat**	sales
سكون/هدوء	**sokoon/hodoo'**	silence/quiet
تواليت/مرحاض	**towaaleet/ merHaaD**	toilets
الخزينة	**al-khazeenah**	till
ساعات الزيارة	**saAat az-zayaarah**	visiting hours
دخول	**dokhool**	way in/entrance
خروج	**khorooj**	way out
إحذر الدهان	**eHzar ad-dehaan**	wet paint

DAYS, MONTHS, SEASONS

Sunday	yawm al-aHad
Monday	yawm al-ethnayn
Tuesday	yawm ath-tholatha'
Wednesday	yawm al-arbeAa'
Thursday	yawm al-khamees
Friday	yawm al-jomAh
Saturday	yawm as-sabt
January	yanaayer
February	febraayer
March	maars
April	ebreel
May	maayo
June	yoonyo
July	yoolyo
August	aghosTos
September	sebtember
October	oktoober
November	noofember
December	deesember
Spring	al-ar-rabeeA
Summer	aS-Sayf
Autumn	al-khareef
Winter	ash-sheta'
Christmas	al-kreesmaas
Christmas Eve	laylat al-kreesmass
New Year	ra'es as-sanah
New Year's Eve	laylat ra'es as-sanah
Aeed alfeTr	feast at the end of Ramadan
awwal moHarram	Moslem New Year's Day
mawlood al nabee	Mohammed's birthday
ramaDaan	Ramadan (Moslem month of fasting)

NUMBERS, THE CALENDAR

0	·	Sefr	22	٢٢	ethnayn wa Aeshreen
1	١	waaHed	30	٣·	thalaatheen
2	٢	ethnayn	31	٣١	waaHed wa thalaatheen
3	٣	thalaathah	32	٣٢	ethnayn wa thalaatheen
4	٤	arbaAh	40	٤·	arbaAeen
5	٥	khamsah	50	٥·	khamseen
6	٦	settah	60	٦·	setteen
7	٧	sabAh	70	٧·	sabAeen
8	٨	thamaaneeyah	80	٨·	thamaaneen
9	٩	tesAh	90	٩·	tesAeen
10	١·	Asharah	100	١··	me'ah
11	١١	Hedaash	110	١١·	me'ah wa Asharah
12	١٢	etnaash	200	٢··	me'tayn
13	١٣	thalaathaash	300	٣··	thalaathme'ah
14	١٤	arbaAtaash	400	٤··	arbaAme'ah
15	١٥	khamastaash	500	٥··	khamsme'ah
16	١٦	settaash	600	٦··	setme'ah
17	١٧	sabaAtaash	700	٧··	sabAme'ah
18	١٨	thamaantaash	800	٨··	thamaanme'ah
19	١٩	tesAtaash	900	٩··	tesAme'ah
20	٢·	Aeshreen	1000	١···	alf
21	٢١	waaHed wa Aeshreen	2000	٢···	alfayn

10,000 ١٠٠٠٠ Asharat aalaaf

1,000,000 ١٠٠٠٠٠٠ malyoon

You will notice that, while Arabic words are written from right to left, Arabic numerals are written from left to right. You will also notice that a comma is used as a decimal point as well as to show thousands.

THE CALENDAR

1st	al-awal	**16th**	as-saades Ashar
2nd	ath-thaanee	**17th**	as-saabeA Ashar
3rd	ath-thaaleth	**18th**	ath-thaamen Ashar
4th	ar-raabeA	**19th**	at-taaseA Ashar
5th	al-khaames	**20th**	al-Aeshroon
6th	as-saades	**21st**	al-Haadee wa al-Aeshroon
7th	as-saabeA	**22nd**	ath-thaanee wa al-Aeshroon
8th	ath-thaamen	**23rd**	ath-thaaleth wa al-Aeshroon
9th	at-taaseA	**24th**	ar-raabeA wa al-Aeshroon
10th	al-Aashar	**25th**	al khaames wa al-Aeshroon
11th	al-Haadee Ashar	**26th**	as-saades wa al-Aeshroon
12th	ath-thaanee Ashar	**27th**	as-saabeA wa al-Aeshroon
13th	ath-thaaleth ashar	**28th**	ath-thaamen wa al-Aeshroon
14th	ar-raabeA Ashar	**29th**	at-taaseA wa al-Aeshroon
15th	al-khaames Ashar	**30th**	ath-thalaathoon
		31st	al-Haadee wa ath-thalaathoon

16

TIME

today	al-yawm
yesterday	ams
tomorrow	bokrah
the day before yesterday	awal ams
the day after tomorrow	baAd bokrah
this week	haza al-osbooA
last week	al-osbooA al maaDee
next week	al-osbooA al-qaadem
this morning	haza aS-SabaaH
this afternoon	al-yawm baAd aZ-Zohr
this evening	haza al-masa'
tonight	al-laylah
yesterday afternoon	ams baAd aZ-Zohr
last night	laylat ams
tomorrow morning	bokrah feeS-SabaaH
tomorrow night	bokrah feel-masa'
in three days	fee khelaal thalaathat ayaam
three days ago	monzo thalaathat ayaam
late	mota'akhar
early	badree
soon	qareeban
later on	baAdayn
at the moment	al-Heen
second	thaaneeyah
minute	daqeeqah
one minute	daqeeqah waaHedah
two minutes	daqeeqatayn
quarter of an hour	robA saAh
half an hour	noSf saAh
three quarters of an hour	saAh ela robA
hour	saAh
that day	daak al-yawm
every day	kol yawm
all day	Towaal al-yawm

the next day	al-yawm at-taalee

TELLING THE TIME

To say "the time is X o'clock" you simply use the words "as-saAh" followed by the number of the hour. For example, "it is nine o'clock" is "as-saAh tesAh" and "it is five o'clock" is "as-saAh khamsah".

To say it is quarter past the hour you add the words "wa robA" (and a quarter) to the hour. To say it is twenty past the hour you add the words "wa thulth" (and a third) to the hour. To say it is half past you add the words "wa noSf" (and a half) to the hour just passed.

Times between half past and the following hour use the following hour as a base. "Wa" becomes "ela" (minus). "It is twenty to three" is "as-saAh thalaathah ela thulth" (it is three o'clock minus a third). Similarly a quarter to the hour is expressed by the word for that hour with the words "ela robA" (minus a quarter).

To give the time to the minute you either add "wa X daqaa'eq" for times up to the half hour or use the following hour and "ela X daqaa'eq" if the time is between the half hour and the following hour.

The twenty-four hour clock is only used by the military in Arab countries. To make it clear that a time is in the morning you can add "SabaaHan". For the afternoon you can use "baAd aZ-Zohr". Times in the evening may be made unambiguous by adding "masa'an".

am	SabaaHan
pm	baAd aZ-Zohr
one o'clock	as-saAh al-waaHedah
ten past one	waaHedah wa Asharah
quarter past one	waaHedah wa robA
half past one	waaHedah wa noSf
twenty to two	ethnayn ela thulth
quarter to two	ethnayn ela robA
two o'clock	as-saAh al-ethnayn

13.00	as-saAh al-waaHedah baAd aZ-Zohr
16.30	as-saAh al-arbaAh wa noSf
at half past five	as-saAh al-khamsah wa noSf
at seven o'clock	as-saAh sabAh
noon	as-saAh ethnaash Zohran
midnight	as-saAh ethnaash masa'an

HOTELS

The business traveller in the Arab world will have no difficulty in finding suitable accommodation in any Arab country. All major cities have at least one high-quality hotel – at least three-star equivalent – but it is absolutely vital to make a reservation beforehand. If you just turn up on spec you risk having to move to another city for want of alternative accommodation. These quality hotels levy a service charge of between 10% and 15% which is added to the bill, and bell-hops and waiters should be tipped separately. It is worth knowing that there is a particularly hefty mark-up on outgoing telephone and telex calls, particularly international ones, and you might wish to avoid this burden by being called instead. Some of the smaller states such as Qatar, Kuwait and Oman have only this type of quality hotel. Foreign visitors are almost exclusively business travellers and hence there has been no demand for more modest accommodation facilities.

In those countries – such as Egypt, Syria, Jordan, Iraq, Morocco and Tunisia – which have a well-developed tourist industry there is a much wider choice of accommodation to suit all pockets. Hotels range from the luxurious to the very very basic. It is fair to say that if a hotel can be pre-booked from abroad then it is likely to meet minimum standards of hygiene and comfort.

The traveller who is back-packing or on a modest budget will find no shortage of cheap hotel accommodation in these countries. Hotels are usually grouped together in one part of town and it is always best to spend as much as possible on accommodation to ensure that your stay is as pleasant as you can afford.

While English is always spoken in the very large hotels, you will find that you really do need a phrase book in medium and small establishments, particularly away from larger towns and cities. Bon voyage and good luck!

USEFUL WORDS AND PHRASES

balcony	balak<u>oo</u>nah
bathroom	Ham<u>aa</u>m
bed	sar<u>ee</u>r
bedroom	gh<u>o</u>rfat nawm
bill	f<u>aa</u>t<u>oo</u>rah
breakfast	foT<u>oo</u>r
dining room	gh<u>o</u>rfat as-s<u>o</u>frah
dinner	Ash<u>aa</u>'
double room	gh<u>o</u>rf<u>a</u>h mozd<u>a</u>wajah
foyer	S<u>aa</u>lah
full board	eq<u>aa</u>mah kaam<u>e</u>lah
half board	ne<u>s</u>f eq<u>aa</u>mah
hotel	fondoq
key	meft<u>aa</u>H
lift	me<u>s</u>Ad
lounge	S<u>aa</u>lah
lunch	gh<u>a</u>d<u>aa</u>'
manager	mod<u>ee</u>r
reception	esteqb<u>aa</u>l
receptionist	mowa<u>zz</u>af al-esteqb<u>aa</u>l
restaurant	maT<u>A</u>m
room	gh<u>o</u>rfah
room service	kh<u>e</u>dmat al-gh<u>o</u>raf
shower	dosh
single room	gh<u>o</u>rfah be-sar<u>ee</u>r w<u>aa</u>Hed
toilet	tow<u>aa</u>leet
twin room	gh<u>o</u>rfah be-sar<u>ee</u>rayn

Have you any vacancies?
fee <u>A</u>ndak gh<u>o</u>raf khaal<u>ee</u>yah?

I have a reservation
<u>A</u>ndee Hajz

21

HOTELS

I'd like a single room
oreed ghorfah be-sareer waaHed

I'd like a double room
oreed ghorfah mozdawajah

I'd like a twin room
oreed ghorfah be-sareerayn

I'd like a room with a bathroom
oreed ghorfah be-Hammaam

I'd like a room with a balcony
oreed ghorfah be-balakoonah

I'd like a room for one night
oreed ghorfah le-modat laylah waaHedah

I'd like a room for three nights
oreed ghorfah le-modat thalaath layaalee

What is the charge per night?
kam seAr al-ghorfah le-modat laylah waaHedah?

Can I see the room?
momken ashoof al-ghorfah?

I don't know yet how long I'll stay
ma aAref beD-Dabt modat al-eqaamah

When is breakfast?
mata meAad al-foToor?

When is dinner?
mata meAad al-Ashaa'?

22

Would you have my luggage brought up?
momken torsel shonaTee fawq?

Please call me at ... o'clock
law samaHt taSel bee as-saAh ...

Can I have breakfast in my room?
momken tajeeb lee al-foToor fee ghorfatee?

I'll be back at ... o'clock
sa-arjaA as-saAh ...

My room number is ...
ghorfatee raqm ...

I'm leaving tomorrow
ana maashee bokrah

Can I have the bill please?
momken al-faatoorah law samaHt?

I'll pay by credit card
sa-adfaA al-faatoorah Visa, Access

I'll pay cash
sa-adfaA naqdan

Can you get me a taxi?
momken tajeeb lee taaksee?

Can you recommend another hotel?
momken towsee be-fondoq aakhar?

There's no water
ma fee miyaah

There's no toilet paper
ma fee waraq towaaleet

THINGS YOU'LL SEE

حمَـام	**Hammaam**	bath
مبيت وفطور	**mabeet wa foToor**	bed and breakfast
فاتورة	**faatoorah**	bill
فطور	**foToor**	breakfast
مخرج الطوارىء	**makhraj aT-Tawaare'**	emergency exit
اقامة كاملة	**eqaamah kaamelah**	full board
الطابق الأرضي	**aT-Taabeq al-arDee**	ground floor
نصف إقامة	**nesf eqaamah**	half board
مصعد	**mesAd**	lift
غداء	**ghadaa'**	lunch
كل الغرف محجوزة	**kol al-ghoraf maHjoozah**	no vacancies
رقم	**raqam**	number
اسحب	**esHab**	pull
ادفع	**edfaA**	push
استقبال	**esteqbaal**	reception
حجز	**Hazj**	reservation →

24

مطعم	**maTAam**	restaurant
غرفة	**ghorfah**	room
دوش	**dosh**	shower
توالیت/مرحاض	**towaaleet/ merHaaD**	toilet

THINGS YOU'LL HEAR

ana mota'assef, kol al-ghoraf maHjoozah
I'm sorry, we're full

ma fee ghoraf be-sareer waaHed baaqeeyah
There are no single rooms left

ma fee ghoraf be-sareerayn baaqeeyah
There are no double rooms left

le-modat kam laylah?
For how many nights?

shoo esmak?
What is your name?

kayf be-tadfaA al-faatoorah?
How will you be paying?

law samaHt edfaA moqadaman
Please pay in advance

momken ashoof jawaazak law samaHt?
Can I see your passport please?

MOTORING

Visitors to the Arab world often hire cars to get around. The rule of the road everywhere is to drive on the right. Some countries accept a British driving licence for a short period (1-2 months), others require an International driving licence while a few insist on a driver obtaining a temporary national licence locally. In Saudi Arabia women are not permitted to drive on their own except within foreign compounds and it is not recommended anywhere at all. Full and up-to-date details of local requirements can always be obtained from an embassy or consulate of the relevant Arab country abroad, or from a national motoring organisation (such as the AA or the RAC in Britain) or from an international travellers' organisation such as American Express or Thomas Cook & Sons. Although third party insurance is not always compulsory a prudent driver will never drive without cover – inability to pay damages has resulted in a prison sentence in many cases in the past.

Motorways and expressways linking major cities are kept in a fairly good state of repair but once you drive off these main routes you will find that road-repairing and general road maintenance is patchy and frequently non-existent. Traffic control tends to be carried out in cities by human agency as well as traffic-lights – often a combination of both. Traffic police are more in evidence in Arab countries than in Europe and North America and you can be fined on the spot for traffic offences – chiefly speeding.

You will find that motorists use their horns a great deal in traffic jams and at intersections and you will need to acquire this habit to hold your own on the roads.

SOME COMMON ROAD SIGNS

شارع غير مرصوف	**shaareA ghayr marSoof**	bad surface →

26

احترس من القطارات	eHtares min al-qeTaaraat	beware of the trains
موقف سيارات	mawqef sayaaraat	car park
عبور غنم وأبقار	Aoboor ghanam wa abqaar	cattle crossing
احترس	eHtaris	caution
تقاطع طرق	taqaaToA Toroq	crossroads
جمرك	jomrok	customs
خطر	khaTar	danger
منحنى خطر	monHana khaTar	dangerous bend
ملتقى طرق خطر	moltaqa Toroq khaTar	dangerous junction
تحويلة	taHweelah	diversion
نهاية طريق السفر	nehaayat Tareeq as-safar	end of motorway
اسعافات أولية	esAafaat awaleeyah	first-aid
للسيارات الثقيلة	les-sayaaraat ath-thaqeelah	for heavy vehicles
جراج	garaaj	garage
افسح الطريق	efsaH aT-Tareeq	give way
إطفي المصابيح الأمامية	eTfee al-maSaabeeH al-amaameeyah	headlights off

→

أشعل المصابيح الأمامية	ashAel al-maSaabeeh al-amaameeyah	headlights on
تقاطع مستوى	taqaaToA mostawee	level crossings
انعطاف عربات النقل	enAeTaaf Arabaat an-naql	lorries turning
طريق سفر (تدفع فيه الرسوم)	Tareeq safar (todfaA feehee ar-rosoom)	motorway (with toll)
ممنوع الدخول	mamnooA ad-dokhool	no entry
ممنوع التخطي	mamnooA at-takhaTe	no overtaking
ممنوع الوقوف	mamnooA al-woqoof	no parking
ممنوع التجاوز	mamnooA at-tajaawoz	no trespassing
شارع اتجاه واحد	shaareA ettejaah waaHed	one-way street
موقف السيارات	mawqef as-sayaaraat	parking
مشاه	moshaah	pedestrians
بنزين	banzeen	petrol
محطة بنزين	maHaTTat banzeen	petrol station

→

منطقة وقوف محددة	menTaqat woqoof moHaddadah	restricted parking zone
اشغال طرق	ashghaal Toroq	roadworks
مدرسة	madrasah	school
محطة خدمة	maHaTTat khedmah	service station
هدىء السرعة	hadee' as-sorAh	slow
قف	qeff	stop!
نفق	nafaq	subway
رسوم	rosoom	toll
وسط المدينة	wasaT al-madeenah	town centre
شارع غير مستو	shaareA ghayr mostawee	uneven surface

USEFUL WORDS AND PHRASES

automatic	awtoomaateek
boot	shanTat as-sayaarah
breakdown	AoTol
brake	faraamel
car	sayaarah
caravan	karaavaan
clutch	debreeyaaj
crossroads	taqaaToA
to drive	yasooq
engine	moHarrek
exhaust	shakmaan

29

fanbelt	sayr al-marwaHah
garage *(for repairs)*	garaaj meekaaneekee
(for petrol)	maHaTTat banzeen
gear(s)	geer
junction (motorway)	taqaaToA
licence	rokhSah
lights *(head)*	anwaar amaameeyah
(rear)	anwaar khalfeeyah
lorry	looree
manual	Aadee
mirror	meraayah
motorbike	mootooseekl
motorway	Tareeq safar
number plate	lawHat arqaam
petrol	banzeen
road	Tareeq
to skid	yazleq
spares	qeTaA ghiyaar
speed	sorAah
speed limit	Had as-sorAah
speedometer	Adaad as-sorAah
steering wheel	derekseeyoon
to tow	yasHab
traffic lights	eshaaraat moroor
trailer	maqToorah
tyre	taayer
van	sayaarah vaan
wheel	Ajalah
windscreen	zojaaj
windscreen wipers	massaaHaat zojaaj as-sayaarah

I'd like some petrol/oil/water
oreed banzeen/zayt/miyaah

Fill her up please
fawelha law samaHt!

I'd like 10 litres of petrol
oreed Asharah leeter banzeen

Would you check the tyres please?
momken toshayek at-tawaayer law samaHt?

Where can I park?
wayn owaqqef as-sayaarah?

Can I park here?
momken owaqqef as-sayaarah hona?

Is this the road to ...?
hal haza howa aT-Tareeq le ...?

Where is the nearest garage?
wayn aqrab garaaj?

DIRECTIONS YOU MAY BE GIVEN

seedah	straight on
Ala al-yasaar	on the left
leff yasaar	turn left
Ala al-yameen	on the right
leff yameen	turn right
awal shaareA Ala al yameen	first on the right
thaanee shaareA Ala al-yasaar	second on the left
baAd al ...	past the ...

31

Do you do repairs?
hal toSaleHoon sayaaraat?

Can you repair the clutch?
hal taqdar toSalleH ad-debreeyaaj?

How long will it take?
qad aysh waqt be-taakhoz?

There is something wrong with the engine
fee khalal feel-moHarrek

The engine is overheating
al-moHarrek be-taskhan ziyaadah An al-lozoom

The brakes are binding
al-faraamel qaabeDah

I need a new tyre
oreed taayer jadeed

I'd like to hire a car
oreed asta'jer sayaarah

Is there a mileage charge?
hal honaak ajer le kol meel?

THINGS YOU'LL HEAR

hal toreed sayaarah awtoomaateek wala Aadeeyah?
Would you like an automatic or a manual?

momken ashoof rokhsatak?
May I see your licence?

THINGS YOU'LL SEE

الطريق البطيء	**aT-Tareeq al-baTee'**	crawler lane
ديزل	**deezel**	diesel
تحويلة	**taHweelah**	diversion
خروج	**khorooj**	exit
سوبر	**sooper**	four star
طريق سفر	**Tareeq safar**	motorway
مفترق طريق السفر	**moftareq Tareeq as-safar**	motorway junction
زيت	**zayt**	oil
مستوى الزيت	**mostawa az-zayt**	oil level
طابور	**Taaboor**	queue
تصليح	**tasleeH**	repair
سوبر	**sooper**	three star
أزمة مرور	**azmat moroor**	traffic jam
عادي	**Aadee**	two star
هواء الاطارات	**hawaa' al-iTaaraat**	tyre pressure

RAIL TRAVEL

The quality, or even existence, of rail travel varies greatly in the Arab world. With the exception of Saudi Arabia there are no railways at all in the states of the peninsula: the Yemens, Oman, the United Arab Emirates, Qatar, Bahrain and Kuwait. In Saudi Arabia there is one express railway line linking the capital Riyadh and the Arabian Gulf port of Damman. This train carries air-conditioned coaches and provides a comfortable ride into the oil-producing region of the country.

In Jordan, Syria, Lebanon and Iraq there are passenger rail services but these are slow, irregular and rarely air-conditioned. They are much used by local people and are very cheap. If you want to travel a little faster you could use the bus and coach services available in those countries. There are also shared taxi services which ply between the larger towns and cities.

The same situation is true of almost all North African Arab states: Morocco, Algeria, Tunisia and Libya.

When it comes to travel by rail in the Arab world, Egypt wins all the prizes. It has a marvellous railway service which has as its main route a line running from the Mediterranean port of Alexandria, through the capital Cairo, through the ancient city of Luxor near the Valley of the Kings right up to the southern town of Aswan at the foot of the great Nile dams. First class travel, which is extremely cheap compared to Western services, is recommended since it is completely air-conditioned and equals European services in every regard: speed, comfort and restaurant facilities. Whichever class you decide to travel you will find the trains punctual and the trip affords the traveller spectacular views of the Nile scenery and landscape. Travellers to Egypt who have any time to spare really should make an effort to travel on at least part of the Nile-side railway. One of the best ways of making a trip up the Nile is to take the train one way and either fly back if you are short of time or take a felucca (sailing boat) or a Nile steamer taking in a different selection of archaeological attractions which are less easy to get to by train.

In Saudi Arabia women should not travel unaccompanied by a man and elsewhere women should not travel alone by rail – this is true even in Egypt. The reason is not that women may be bothered by men, but that Arab custom does not like to see women out on their own. You will find different ticket counters for men and women in many railway stations.

USEFUL WORDS AND PHRASES

air-conditioning	takyeef al-hawaa'
booking office	maktab Hajz at-tazaaker
buffet	boofay
carriage	Arabah
compartment	maqSoorah
connection	tawSeelah
dining car	Arabat al-ghazaa'
emergency brake	selselah le-tawqeef al-qeTaar
engine	qaaTerah
entrance	madkhal
exit	makhraj
first class	darajah oolah
to get in	yaSAd
to get out	yanzel
guard	Haares
indicator board	lawHat al-bayaanaat
left luggage	maktab al-Haqaa'eb al-matrookah
lost property	al-mafqoodaat
luggage trolley	Arabah Sagheerah le-naql al-Haqaa'eb
luggage van	Arabat naql al-Haqaa'eb
platform	raSeef
pullman	looks
railway	sekkah Hadeedeeyah
reserved seat	maqAd maHjooz
restaurant car	Arabat al-maTAm
return ticket	tazkarat zehaab wa Awdah

35

RAIL TRAVEL

seat	maqAd
second class	darajah thaaneeyah
single ticket	tazkarat zehaab faqaT
sleeping car	Arabat nawm
station	maHaTTah
station master	naazer al-maHaTTah
ticket	tazkarah
ticket collector	moHaSSel at-tazaaker
timetable	jadwal mawaAeed
tracks	qoDbaan
train	qeTaar
waiting room	ghorfat al-entezaar
window	shobbaak

When does the train for ... leave?
emta yaqoom al-qeTaar ellee raayeH le ...?

When does the train from ... arrive?
emta yaSel al-qeTaar ellee jaay men ...?

When is the next train to ...?
emta al-qeTaar at-taalee le ...?

When is the first/last train to ...?
emta awal/aakher qeTaar le ...?

What is the fare to ...?
be-kam at-tazkarah le ...?

Do I have to change?
hal laazem oghayyer al-qeTaar?

Does the train stop at ...?
hal al-qeTaar yaqef fee maHaTTat ...?

How long does it take to get to ...?
aysh Tool al-masaafah le ...?

A single ticket to ... please
law samaHt, tazkarat zehaab le ...

A return ticket to ... please
law samaHt, tazkarat zehaab wa Awdah le ...

Do I have to pay a supplement?
hal laazem adfaA mablagh eDaafee?

I'd like to reserve a seat
oreed aHjez maqAd law samaHt

Is this the right train for ...?
hal haza howa al-qeTaar le ...?

Is this the right platform for the ... train?
hal haza howa ar-raSeef lel-qeTaar ...?

Which platform for the ... train?
wayn ar-raseef lel-qeTaar ellee raayeH ...?

Is the train late?
hal al-qeTaar mota'akhar?

Could you help me with my luggage please?
momken tosaAednee fee shayl shonaTee law samaHt?

Is this a non-smoking compartment?
hal hazehe maqSoorah mamnooA feeha at-tadkheen?

Is this seat free?
hal haza al-maqAd khaalee?

37

RAIL TRAVEL

This seat is taken
haza al-maqAd mashghool

I have reserved this seat
ana Hajazet haza al-maqAd

May I open/close the window?
momken aftaH/aqfel ash-shobbaak?

When do we arrive in ...?
emta naSel ...?

What station is this?
hazehe ay maHaTTah?

Do we stop at ...?
hal al-qeTaar yaqef fee maHaTTat ...?

Would you keep an eye on my things for a moment?
momken tokhalee baalak men shonaTee law samaHt?

Is there a restaurant car on this train?
hal fee Arabat maTAm fee haza al-qeTaar?

THINGS YOU'LL SEE

الوصول	**al-woSool**	arrivals
عربة	**Arabah**	carriage
المحطة المركزية	**al-maHaTTah al-markazeeyah**	central station
تغيير عملة	**taghyeer Aomlah**	currency exchange
تأخير	**ta'akheer**	delay

رحيل	**raHeel**	departures
لا يقف في ...	**laa yaqef fee ...**	does not stop in ...
لا تطل برأسك خارج الشباك	**laa taTol be-ra'esak khaarej ash-shobbaak**	do not lean out of the window
سلسلة لتوقيف القطار	**selselah le-tawqeef al-qeTaar**	emergency brake
مشغول	**mashghool**	engaged
مدخل	**madkhal**	entrance
مخرج	**makhraj**	exit
معلومات	**maAloomaat**	information
رحلة	**reHlah**	journey
حقائب متروكة	**Haqaa'eb matrookah**	left luggage
قطار محلي	**qeTaar maHallee**	local train
دكان بيع الجرائد	**dokaan bayA al-jaraa'id**	newspaper kiosk
ممنوع الدخول	**mamnooA ad-dokhool**	no entry
غرامة للاستخدام الخطىء	**gharaamah lel-estekhdaam al-khaTa'**	penalty for misuse
رصيف	**raSeef**	platform
تذكرة رصيف	**tazkarat raSeef**	platform ticket
طريق	**Tareeq**	road →

39

حجز المقاعد	**Hajz al-maqaAed**	seat reservation
عربة نوم	**Arabat nawm**	sleeping car
مدخنون	**modakhenoon**	smokers
وجبات خفيفة	**wajabaat khafeefah**	snacks
شارع	**shaareA**	street
تكملة	**takmelah**	supplement
تذاكر/مكتب حجز التذاكر	**tazaaker/maktab Hajz at-tazaaker**	tickets/ticket office
مكتب التذاكر	**maktab at-tazaaker**	ticket office
جدول المواعيد	**jadwal al-mawaAeed**	timetable
إلى القطارات	**ela al-qeTaaraat**	to the trains
خالي	**khaalee**	vacant
غرفة الانتظار	**ghorfat al-enteZaar**	waiting room

THINGS YOU'LL HEAR

entebaah
Attention

at-tazaaker law samaHt
Tickets please

AIR TRAVEL

All Arab countries have air links with the outside world. In fact some, like North Yemen, are virtually inaccessible except by air. Many of the larger countries, particularly Saudi Arabia, have an efficient and modern internal service. As most travellers will arrive in their country of destination by air here is the place to give a word of warning: almost all Arab states have strict visa requirements for passport-holders from European and North American countries as well as Australia and New Zealand, and visas must very often be obtained from that country's embassy or consulate in the traveller's country of residence. Travellers without the correct visa may be refused entry. Do not travel to any Arab country other than Egypt with a passport containing Israeli stamps. Some countries, such as Saudi Arabia, will confiscate any alcohol or unsuitable literature you may be carrying, and the penalties for smuggling any types of illicit drugs are among the heaviest in the world. In common with many countries Arab police are particularly sensitive about 'plane spotters' and anyone photographing airports and aircraft. So use your common sense and don't risk being branded a spy.

USEFUL WORDS AND PHRASES

aircraft	Tayaarah
air hostess	moDeefah jaweeyah
airline	khaT Tayaraan
airport	maTaar
airport bus	baaS al-maTaar
aisle	mamsha yafSel bayn al-karaasee
arrival	woSool
baggage claim	akhz al-Haqaa'eb
boarding card	beTaaqat aS-SoAood leT-Taa'erah
check-in	at-tasjeel wa ad-dokhool
check-in desk	maktab tasjeel wa dokhool ar-rokaab

customs	jomrok
delay	ta'akheer
departure	raHeel
departure lounge	qaAt ar-raHeel
emergency exit	makhraj aT-Tawaare'
flight	reHlah
flight number	raqam ar-reHlah
gate	bawaabah
jet	jet
to land	yahboT
long distance flight	reHlat Tayaraan le-masaafah Taweelah
passport	jawaaz safar
passport control	moraaqabat al-jawaazaat
pilot	Tayaar
runway	madraj aT-Taa'eraat
seat	maqAd
seat belt	Hezaam al-maqAd
steward	moDeef
stewardess	moDeefah
take-off	eqlaA
visa	veeza
window	shobbaak
wing	janaaH

When is there a flight to ...?
emta be-yakoon fee reHlat Tayaraan le ...?

What time does the flight to ... leave?
emta mawAed eqlaA Tayaarat ...?

Is it a direct flight?
hal heya reHlah mobaasherah?

Do I have to change planes?
hal laazem oghayyer aT-Tayaarah?

When do I have to check in?
emta be-yakoon fee tasjeel ar-rokaab

I'd like a single ticket to ...
oreed tazkarat zehaab le ...

I'd like a return ticket to ...
oreed tazkarat zehaab wa Awdah le ...

I'd like a non-smoking seat please
oreed maqAd feel-joz' elee mamnooA feehee at-tadkheen law
samaHt

I'd like a window seat please
oreed maqAd janb ash-shobbaak law samaHt

How long will the flight be delayed?
kam modat ta'akheer ar-reHlah?

Is this the right gate for the ... flight?
hal hazi al-bawaabah aS-SaHeeHah le-reHlat ...?

Which gate for the flight to ...?
ay bawaabah le-reHlat ...?

When do we arrive in ...?
emta naSel le ...?

May I smoke now?
momken odakhen seejaarah al-Heen?

I don't feel very well
ana mareeD shway

43

THINGS YOU'LL SEE

طيارة	**Tayaarah**	aircraft
الوصول	**al-wosool**	arrivals
أخذ الحقائب	**akhz al-Haqaa'eb**	baggage claim
تسجيل ودخول الركاب	**tasjeel wa dokhool ar-rokaab**	check-in
يسجل	**yesajjil**	to check-in
جمارك	**jamaarek**	customs
مراقبة الجمارك	**moraaqabat al-jamaarek**	customs control
تأخير	**ta'akheer**	delay
رحيل	**raHeel**	departures
رحلة مباشرة	**reHlah mobaasherah**	direct flight
مخرج الطوارىء	**makhraj aT-Tawaare'**	emergency exit
هبوط إضطراري	**hoboot eDTeraaree**	emergency landing
اربط أحزمة المقاعد	**erboT aHzemat al-maqaAed**	fasten seat belt
رحلة	**reHlah**	flight
بوابة	**bawaabah**	gate
معلومات	**maAloomaat**	information →

44

هبوط	**hoboot**	landing
التوقيت المحلي	**at-tawqeet al-maHallee**	local time
لغير المدخنين	**le-ghayr al-modakheneen**	non-smokers
الرجاء الامتناع عن التدخين	**ar-rejaa' al-emtenaA An at-tadkheen**	no smoking please
ركاب	**rokaab**	passengers
مراقبة جوازات السفر	**moraaqabat jawaazaat as-safar**	passport control
رحلة محددة المواعيد	**reHlah moHaddadat al-mawaAeed**	scheduled flight
إقلاع	**eqlaA**	take-off

THINGS YOU'LL HEAR

yaSAd ar-rokaab al-aan ela aT-Taa'erah al-motajehah ela ...
The flight for ... is now boarding

ar-rejaa' at-tawajoh al-aan ela bawaabah raqam ...
Please go now to gate number ...

45

BY BUS AND TAXI

Bus travel is the main way Arabs get around their countries. In the almost complete absence of regular, fast rail services (see BY RAIL for exceptions) cities and towns are linked by regular, usually fast, bus services. Inter-city buses are almost without exception air-conditioned. If the route crosses any desert area, then there will definitely be air-conditioning. Although you can usually buy your ticket as you board the bus you can also buy it at the bus station and this is preferable since it can be done in a more leisurely and accurate way than in a jostling queue pushing to get aboard.

Within the large towns and cities the Westerner may find the buses very overcrowded and slow. Taxi travel may be preferred – they are relatively cheap. There are two types of taxi. One is just as in the West. But although these taxis do sometimes have meters the fare they show is not binding and a prospective passenger is wise to get a firm price out of the driver before setting off.

The other type of taxi is one which plies a fixed route and which can be shared by several passengers getting on and off at different points. These are called 'taaksee ben-nafar'. Using these taxis, however, presupposes that you know where the cab is going. Since they do not carry any signs, only experience of a particular city will tell you this. These taxis are best used only by travellers who have an Arabic-speaking companion with them or who have an adventurous streak in them!

USEFUL WORDS AND PHRASES

adult	baalegh
boat	markeb
bus	baaS
bus stop	maHaTTat baaSaat
child	Tefl
coach	baaS
conductor	moHaSSel tazaaker

connection	tawSeelah
cruise	jawlah baHareeyah
driver	saa'eq
fare	ojrah
ferry	Abaarah
network map	khareeTat al-baaSaat
number 5 bus	baaS raqam khamsah
passenger	raakeb
port	meenaa'
quay	raSeef al-meenaa'
river	nahr
seat	maqAd
station	maHaTTah
subway	nafaq
taxi	taaksee
terminus	maHaTTah nehaa'eeyah
ticket	tazkarah
tram	traam

Where is the bus station?
wayn maHaTTat al-baaSaat?

Where is there a bus stop?
wayn maHaTTat baaSaat qareebah?

Which buses go to ...?
aysh heya al-baaSaat elee tarooH le ...?

How often do the buses to ... run?
kol qad aysh taseer al-baaSaat elee raayeHah ela ...?

Would you tell me when we get to ...?
momken tonabbehnee lama naSel ela ...?

Do I have to get off yet?
hal laazem anzel al-aan?

47

BY BUS AND TAXI

How do you get to ...?
kayf tarooH le ...?

Is it very far?
hal heya baAeedah?

I want to go to ...
oreed arooh le ...

Do you go near ...?
hal taseer bel-qorb men ...?

Where can I buy a ticket?
men wayn ashtaree tazkarah?

Could you open/close the window?
momken teftaH/taqfel ash-shobbaak?

Could you help me get a ticket?
momken taqool lee kayf ajeeb tazkarah?

When does the last bus leave?
emta meeAaad qiyaam aakher baas?

How much will it cost?
qad aysh be-tatakallef?

Can you wait here and take me back?
momken tantaZer hona wa terajaAnee marrah thaanyah?

THINGS YOU'LL SEE

بالغين	**baalegheen**	adults
تكييف الهواء	**takyeef al-hawaa**	air-conditioning
يغير	**yoghayyer**	to change
أطفال	**aTfaal**	children
خروج	**khorooj**	departure, exit
لاتتتحدث مع السائق	**laa tataHaddath maA as-saa'eq**	do not speak to the driver
مخرج الطوارىء	**makhraj aT-Tawaare'**	emergency exit
مدخل	**madkhal**	entrance
الدخول من الأمام/ الخلف	**ad-dokhool men al-amaam/ al-khalf**	entry at the front/rear
كامل العدد	**kaamel al-Adad**	full
ممنوع الدخول	**mamnooA ad-dokhool**	no entry
ممنوع التدخين	**mamnooA at-tadkheen**	no smoking
يدفع	**yadfaA**	to pay
طريق	**Tareeq**	route
مقاعد	**maqaAid**	seats
يعرض	**yaAreD**	to show ➜

يقف	**yaqef**	stop
موقف التاكسيات	**mawqef at-taakseeyaat**	taxi rank
محطة نهائية	**maHaTTah nehaa'eeyah**	terminus
تذكرة	**tazkarah**	ticket

DOING BUSINESS

The Western businessman travelling in the Arab world will find his counterparts both educated and sophisticated. Any idea that Arab business is carried out these days with the medieval conspiracies of the casbah must be utterly dismissed. Today's businessmen in every Arab country are part of the educated elite, often with ties to the political establishment in that country, which controls all major foreign trade dealings of that particular state. These businessmen will have considerable knowledge of Western ways and will often have travelled in Western countries themselves. An important point worth noting is that many businessmen in manufacturing industries in the Arab world are themselves engineers of high calibre and great expertise in their product field. Western companies should ensure that a suitably qualified member of staff is despatched on business in areas requiring technical skill otherwise they may have rings drawn around them by their Arab hosts.

Arab hospitality is renowned throughout the world and rightly so. Western businessmen will find their Arab counterparts open and friendly and genuine friendships will easily be made. Before any business meeting coffee or tea will be served, sweet and without milk and in very small cups. You will be expected to drink two or three of these before finally declining yet another offer of a refill by shaking the empty cup gently from side to side and returning it to your host.

You should always dress particularly neatly and always be on time for appointments. In this regard you should wear a tie and short-sleeved shirt in hot climates and a suit or jacket and tie in cooler environments. You may well find that meetings and appointments do not run to a particularly punishing schedule and, indeed, you should allow for considerable delays in the timetable of events and plan your days accordingly, with room for rearrangement of dislocated events.

When you are introduced to Arab colleagues you should shake them by the hand. If you get to know someone well you may be embraced and even kissed and you should take this in your stride and reciprocate.

If you are invited out to dine with an Arab colleague you will usually be taken out to a restaurant – not to his home. The host always pays for everything and you should not even offer to pay. What you should do however, is to extend your own invitation to your host to dine (at your expense!) in your hotel or a good restaurant you know.

Do not forget that in many Arab countries, such as Saudi Arabia, the United Arab Emirates, Oman and Qatar, alcohol is strictly forbidden. It is certainly frowned upon everywhere in the Arab world. While strong drink is often served in international hotels outside the peninsula, it is wisest to refrain from drinking alcohol at all in the presence of Arab colleagues unless they make it clear they do not object. Your trip to the Arab world is the ideal time to clear your head and give your liver a break.

There are very few businesswomen working as executives in Arab companies and it is fair to say that the Arab world is not the place for Western businesswomen to venture yet. This is certainly true of Saudi Arabia, where women may not even drive a car or travel unescorted by a man, but applies to all Arab countries to a varying degree.

USEFUL WORDS AND PHRASES

accept	yaqbal
accountant	moHaaseb
accounts department	edaarat al-moHaasebah
advertisement	eAlaan
advertising	eAlaanaat
to airfreight	yashHen bel-jaw
bid	ATaa'
board (of directors)	hay'ah
brochure	kotayeb
business card	kaart
businessman	rajol aAmaal
chairman	ra'ees

cheap	rakhee<u>S</u>
client	Amee<u>l</u>
company	she<u>r</u>kah
computer	kompyooter
consumer	mosta<u>h</u>lik
contract	Aqd
cost	takle<u>f</u>ah
customer	zaboon
director	mo<u>d</u>eer
discount	takh<u>feeD</u>
documents	watha<u>a</u>'eq
down payment	Arb<u>oon</u>
engineer	mo<u>h</u>andes
executive	mona<u>ff</u>ez
expensive	ghaa<u>l</u>ee
exports	<u>S</u>aaderaat
fax	faaks
to import	yasta<u>w</u>red
imports	waaredaat
instalment	do<u>f</u>Ah
invoice	faat<u>oo</u>rah
to invoice	yorse<u>l</u> faat<u>oo</u>rah le
letter	khe<u>T</u>aab
letter of credit	khe<u>T</u>a<u>a</u>b eAtem<u>aa</u>d
loss	khosa<u>a</u>rah
manager	mo<u>d</u>eer
manufacture	<u>S</u>an<u>A</u>h
margin	rebH ejm<u>aa</u>lee
market	sooq
marketing	tas<u>w</u>eeq
meeting	ejtemA
negotiations	mofaawa<u>D</u>a<u>a</u>t
offer	Ar<u>D</u>
order	<u>T</u>alab
to order	ya<u>T</u>lob
personnel	<u>h</u>ay'at al-mowa<u>Z</u>af<u>ee</u>n
price	se<u>A</u>r

product	montaj
production	entaaj
profit	rebH
promotion *(publicity)*	tarweej
purchase order	Talab sheraa'
sales department	qesm al-mabeeAat
sales director	modeer mabeeAat
sales figures	arqaam al-mabeeAat
secretary *(male)*	sekretayr
(female)	sekretayrah
shipment	shoHnah
tax	Dareebah
telex	teleks
tender	ATaa' fee monaaqaSah
total	majmooA

My name is ...
esmee ...

Here's my card
tafaDal kaartee

Pleased to meet you
tasharafna be-moqaabelatak

May I introduce ...?
momken oqadem lak ...?

My company is ...
sherkatee esmaha ...

Our product is selling very well in the UK market
beDaAtna Alayha eqbaal shadeed fee aswaaq engeltera

We are looking for partners in the Arab world
neHna be-nabHath An shorakaa' feel-Aalem al-Arabee

At our last meeting ...
fee moqaabelatna al-akheerah ...

10%/25%/50%
Asharah feel-me'ah/khamsah wa Aeshreen feel-me'ah/khamseen feel-me'ah

More than ...
akthar men ...

Less than ...
aqal men ...

We're on schedule
neHna maasheeyeen Hasab al-jadwal tamaaman

We're slightly behind schedule
neHna mota'akhareen qaleelan

Please accept our apologies
arjook eqbaal eAtezaarna

There are good government grants available
fee menaH momtaazah men al-Hokoomah

It's a deal
mowaafeq

I'll have to check that with my chairman
laazem aakhoz ra'y al-modeer al-Aam

I'll get back to you on that
be-arod Alayk qareeban be-khoSooS haza al-mawDooA

Our quote will be with you very shortly
be-norsel lak as-seAr qareeban jeddan

DOING BUSINESS

We'll send it by telex
sa-norselha bet-teleks

We'll send them airfreight
sa-noshHenha beT-Tayaarah

It's a pleasure to do business with you
yosAednee an atAamel maAk

Can we invite you to dinner in our hotel?
momken nadAook lel-Ashaa' fee fondoqna?

We look forward to a mutually beneficial business relationship
atamanna enha takoon Alaaqat Amal mofeedah leT-Tarafayn

RESTAURANTS

All large hotels have a restaurant which serves meals in the Western style, although the menu will probably contain some traditional Arab dishes and some specialities of the region you are in. If you are staying at a smaller hotel without its own restaurant you are sure to find a range of local restaurants covering different price ranges. Restaurants often specialize in dishes based on one type of food: lamb grills, fowl of various kinds or perhaps fish and seafood.

Although most Arab countries serve alcohol in tourist hotels some, such as Saudi Arabia, Qatar and the United Arab Emirates, will not permit anyone to drink alcohol legally anywhere at any time.

Arab cooking is mainly based on mutton, lamb, fish or chicken. Pork is not eaten by Muslims and cooking in wine is rare.

Restaurants are set out as they are in the West and as well as table napkins they often provide finger-bowls. It is considered impolite to smoke during a meal, even in between courses. You will know when the meal is at an end because small cups of bitter coffee are served. It is normal to take two or three of these cups after a meal.

Coffee in the Arab World normally means Turkish coffee, which is taken very strong and black – like an espresso but with cardamom and other spices in it. You can have it three ways: no sugar – saadah; medium – maZbooT; sweet – sokkar zeyaadah.

Apart from conventional Western-style restaurants you can also eat out at a snack-bar (kaafeterya) where cheaper salad-type dishes are served, often based on beans or spicy fried chickpea balls.

In all major towns there will also be kiosks selling glasses of fruit juice or canned drinks and biscuits and crisps.

USEFUL WORDS AND PHRASES

beer	beerah
bottle	zojaajah
cake	kayk
coffee	qahwah
cup	fenjaan

RESTAURANTS

fork	shawkah
glass	koob
knife	sekeen
menu	qaa'emat aT-TAam
milk	Haleeb
plate	Tabaq
sandwich	sandwetsh
snack	wajbah khafeefah
soup	shorbah
spoon	malAaqah
sugar	sukkar
table	Taawlah
tea	shaay
tip	baqsheesh
water	miyaah
white coffee	qahwah bel-Haleeb
wine	nabeez
wine list	qaa'emat an-nabeez

A table for one please
Taawlah le-shakhS waaHed law samaHt

A table for two please
Taawlah le-shakhSayn law samaHt

Can I see the menu?
momken ashoof qaa'emat aT-TAam law samaHt?

What would you recommend?
tawsee be-ay nawA?

I'd like ...
oreed ...

Just a cup of coffee, please
fenjaan qahwah faqaT, law samaHt

Waiter/waitress!
ya garsoon/ya garsoonah!

Can we have the bill, please?
momken al-Hesaab, law samaHt?

Is there a set menu?
hal fee qaa'emah moHaddadah?

I didn't order this
ana ma Talabt haza

May we have some more ...?
momken shewayah kaman ... law samaHt?

The meal was very good, thank you
al-wajbah kaanat momtaazah, shokran

My compliments to the chef!
teslam eed aT-Tabaakh!

YOU MAY HEAR

bel-hanaa' wash-shefaa'!
Enjoy your meal!

YOU MAY SEE

مطعم **maTAam** restaurant

MENU READER

STARTERS, SOUPS & SALADS

سلاطة باذنجان	**salaaTat baazenjaan**	aubergine salad
بورك	**boorek**	'bourek' – savoury pastry
كافيار	**kaafiyaar**	caviar
حامض	**HaamoD**	chicken and vegetable soup with lemon
شوربة دجاج	**shoorbat dajaaj**	chicken soup
شوربة صافية	**shorbah Saafeeyah**	consommé
تبولة	**taboolah**	cracked wheat salad
فتة	**fattah**	festival soup – with lamb, rice and tomato
شوربة سمك	**shoorbat samak**	fish soup
عصير فاكهة	**ASeer faakehah**	fruit juice
حنود شامي	**Hanood shaamee**	garlic and rice salad
سلاطة خضراء	**salaaTah khaDra'**	green salad
حمص	**HommoS**	'hummous' – puréed chickpeas
شوربة عدس	**shoorbat Adas**	lentil soup
شمام	**shammaam**	melon

60

زيتون	**zaytoon**	olives
سلاطة شرقية	**salaaTah sharqeeyah**	Oriental mixed vegetable salad
باتيه	**paateeh**	pâté
مخللات	**mekhallalaat**	pickles
سلاطة بطاطس	**salaaTat baTaaTes**	potato salad
سلاطة	**salaaTah**	salad
سردين	**sardeen**	sardines
شوربة	**shoorbah**	soup
مزة	**mazzah**	starter
ورق عنب محشي	**waraq Aenab maHshee**	stuffed vine leaves
تبولة	**taboolah**	'taboola' – cracked wheat
طحينة	**TaHeenah**	'tahina' – sesame seed paste
بابا غنوج	**baaba ghanooj**	'tahina' – with aubergine
سلاطة طماطم	**salaaTat TamaaTem**	tomato salad
ملوخية	**molookheeyah**	traditional soup of garlic and greens
شوربة خضار	**shoorbat khoDaar**	vegetable soup
سلاطة جرجير	**salaaTat jarjeer**	watercress salad
سلاطة خيار باللبن	**salaaTat khiyaar bel-laban**	yoghurt and cucumber salad

EGGS, CHEESE & PASTA

بيض مسلوق	**bayD maslooq**	boiled egg
جبنة	**jebnah**	cheese
لبنة	**labnah**	curd cheese
بيض	**bayD**	egg
مش	**mesh**	firm, salty cheese
بيض مقلي	**bayD maqlee**	fried egg
جبنة رومي	**jebnah roomee**	hard cheese
مكرونة	**makaroonah**	macaroni
كوسة بجبنة	**koosah be-jebnah**	marrow and cheese dish
جبنة قديمة	**jebnah qadeemah**	mature cheese
شعرية	**sheAreeyah**	noodles
عجة	**Aejah**	omelette with onions and parsley
جبنة مالحة	**jebnah maaleHah**	salty cheese
شكشوكة	**shakshookah**	scrambled eggs with mince
جبنة فلاحي	**jebnah falaaHee**	soft cheese
مكرونة سباجتي	**makaroonah spaghetti**	spaghetti
جبنة بيضاء	**jebnah bayDa'**	white cheese

FISH

انشوجة	**anshoogah**	anchovies
شبوط	**shabooT**	carp
كافيار	**kaafiyaar**	caviar
كابوريا	**kaabooriya**	crab
ثعبان الماء	**thoAbaan al-maa'**	eels
سمك	**samak**	fish
ترنشات	**taranshaat**	fish fillets
سمك بزيت	**samak be-zayt**	fish in oil
سمك طرطور	**samak TarToor**	fish with garlic sauce
سمك صيادية	**samak Sayaadeeyah**	fish with rice
سمك مقلي	**samak maqlee**	fried fish
سمك مشوي	**samak mashwee**	grilled fish
كركند	**kerkend**	lobster
استاكوزا	**estakooza**	(in Egypt) lobster
بوري	**booree**	mullet
اخطبوط	**akhTabooT**	octopus
محار	**maHaar**	oysters
فرخ	**farkh**	perch
جمبري	**jambaree**	prawns
سردين	**sardeen**	sardines

سمك مدخن	**samak medakhan**	smoked fish
سمك موسى	**samak moosa**	sole
حبار	**Habaar**	squid
سمك الأطروط	**samak al-aTrooT**	trout
تونة	**toonah**	tuna
سمك الترس	**samak at-ters**	turbot

MEAT & FOWL

لحم بقري	**laHm baqaree**	beef
بفتيك	**boftayk**	beefsteak
صدر	**sadr**	breast
دجاج	**dajaaj**	chicken
كفتة دجاج	**koftat dajaaj**	chicken balls
كستليتة	**kosteleetah**	cutlet
بط	**baTT**	duck
اسكالوب	**eskaaloob**	escalope
فيليتو	**feelett**	fillet
وز	**wezz**	goose
كباب	**kebaab**	grilled lamb on a skewer
حمام مشوي	**Hamaam mashwee**	grilled pigeon
كلاوي	**kalaawee**	kidneys
لحم ضاني	**laHm Daanee**	lamb

ريش ضاني	**reeyash ᴅaanee**	lamb chop
ورك	**werk**	leg
فخذ ضاني	**fakhz ᴅaanee**	leg of lamb
كبدة	**kebdah**	liver
لحم	**laнm**	meat
كفتة	**koftah**	meatballs
لحم مفروم	**laнm mafroom**	minced meat
مشويات متنوعة	**mashweeyaat motanawweeᴀah**	mixed grilled meats
حمام	**наmaam**	pigeon
أرنب	**arnab**	rabbit
روسبيف	**roosbeef**	roast beef
دجاج مشوي	**dajaaj mashwee**	roast chicken
خروف محشي	**kharoof maнshee**	roast lamb on a spit
كتف ضاني	**ketef ᴅaanee**	shoulder of lamb
شاورمة	**shaawerma**	sliced spit-roast lamb
سوجق حار	**sojoq наar**	spicy salami
لحم أوزي	**laнm oozee**	spring lamb
شوا	**shooa**	steamed lamb
مزات	**mozaat**	substantial veal stew
لسان	**lesaan**	tongue
ديك رومي	**deek roomee**	turkey
سجق	**sojoq**	type of sausage
لحم عجل	**laнm ᴀejl**	veal

اسكالوب عجل	**eskaloob Aejl**	veal escalope

MAIN DISHES

مسقعة	**mosaqqAh**	aubergine with raisins and meat
فريك	**fereek**	chicken served with hard-boiled eggs
فراخ شركسية	**feraakh sharkaseeyah**	chicken with rice, chilli and nuts
كشك بالفراخ	**keshk bel-feraakh**	chicken with yoghurt and onion
كسكس	**koos-koos**	'couscous' – lamb and steamed semolina
كباب سمك	**kebaab samak**	grilled fish on a skewer with tomatoes and green peppers
فلافل	**falaafel**	'felafel' – fried balls of ground beans or chickpeas
طعمية	**TaAmeeyah**	fried balls of ground beans with herbs
كشري	**kosharee**	'kosharee' – mixed rice, lentils, pasta and onions in a piquant sauce
لحم ضاني برياني	**laHm Daanee bereeyaanee**	lamb biriyani

مقلوبة	**maql<u>oo</u>bah**	meat stewed with aubergines and rice
كفتة مبرومة	**koftah mabr<u>oo</u>mah**	minced meat with nuts
قدرة فراخ	**qedrat fer<u>aa</u>kh**	North African chicken stew
صفيحة	**saf<u>ee</u>Hah**	pastry base topped with minced lamb
لسان العصفور	**les<u>aa</u>n al-A0Sf<u>oo</u>r**	stewed lamb with vermicelli
دفينة	**daf<u>ee</u>nah**	thick stew of chickpeas and beans

VEGETABLES

خرشوف	**kharsh<u>oo</u>f**	artichokes
الهليون	**al-hely<u>oo</u>n**	asparagus
باذنجان	**baazenj<u>aa</u>n**	aubergine
أبوكادو	**abook<u>aa</u>do**	avocado
فول مدمس	**fool med<u>a</u>mmes**	bean purée
بنجر	**b<u>a</u>njar**	beetroot
فول	**fool**	broad beans
كرنب	**kor<u>o</u>nb**	cabbage
جزر	**j<u>a</u>zar**	carrots
أرنبيط	**arnab<u>ee</u>T**	cauliflower
كرفس	**kar<u>a</u>fs**	celery

فلفل حامي	**felfel Haamee**	chillies
كوسة	**koosah**	courgettes
خيار	**khiyaar**	cucumber
ثوم	**thoom**	garlic
فاصوليا خضراء	**fasooliya khaDra'**	green beans
فاصوليا خضراء بزيت	**fasooliya khaDra' be-zayt**	green beans cooked in oil
فلفل أخضر	**felfel akhDar**	green peppers
فاصوليا	**fasooliya**	haricot beans
طرطوفة	**TarToofah**	Jerusalem artichokes
كراث	**koraath**	leeks
عدس	**Adas**	lentils
خس	**khass**	lettuce
باذنجان مخلل	**baazenjaan mekhallel**	marinated aubergine
بامية	**baameeyah**	okra, ladies' fingers
بصل	**basal**	onions
بازلاء	**baazella**	peas
بطاطس	**baTaaTes**	potatoes
فجل	**fejel**	radishes
رز	**rozz**	rice
سبانخ	**sabaanekh**	spinach
بصل أخضر	**basal akhDar**	spring onions

كرنب محشي	**koronb maHshee**	stuffed cabbage
فلفل محشي	**felfel maHshee**	stuffed peppers
بطاطس محشية	**baTaaTes maHsheeyah**	stuffed potatoes
ذرة	**zorrah**	sweet corn
بطاطا	**baTaaTaa**	sweet potatoes
طماطم	**TamaaTem**	tomatoes
لفت	**left**	turnips
خضار	**khoDaar**	vegetables
طاجن خضار	**Taajen khoDaar**	vegetable stew
جرجير	**jarjeer**	watercress

FRUIT & NUTS

لوز	**looz**	almonds
تفاح	**teffaaH**	apples
مشمش	**meshmesh**	apricots
موز	**mooz**	bananas
توت عليق	**toot Aleeq**	blackberries
الكستناء	**al-kestenaa'**	chestnuts
جوز هند	**jooz hend**	coconut
فواكه مجففة	**fawaakeh mojaffafah**	dried fruit
محمصات	**moHammaSaat**	dried seeds
تين	**teen**	figs

فواكه	**fawaakeh**	fruit
جريب فروت	**grayb froot**	grapefruit
عنب	**Aenab**	grapes
بندق	**bondoq**	hazelnuts
ليمون حامض	**laymoon HaameD**	lemon
ليمون	**laymoon**	limes
مانجة	**maanjah**	mangoes
شمام	**shammaam**	melon
جوز	**jooz**	nuts
برتقال	**bortogaal**	oranges
خوخ	**khookh**	peaches
فول سوداني	**fool soodaanee**	peanuts
كمثري	**komethra**	pears
أناناس	**anaanaas**	pineapple
فستق	**fostoq**	pistachio nuts
برقوق	**barqooq**	plums
زبيب	**zebeeb**	raisins
راوند	**rawand**	rhubarb
فراولة	**farawlah**	strawberries
يسفندي	**yoosefendee**	tangerines
بطيخ	**baTeekh**	watermelon

DESSERTS

سنبوسك باللوز	**senboosak bel-looz**	almond slice
بسكويت	**baskooweet**	biscuits
كيك	**kayk**	cake
كريم كراميل	**kreem karamel**	crème caramel
بلح الشام	**balaH ash-shaam**	'Dates of Damascus' – fried tartlets with syrup
حلويات	**Halawiyaat**	dessert
رز بلبن	**rozz be-laban**	dish of rice with milk and rosewater
خشاف	**khoshaaf**	dish of stewed fruits
كل واشكر	**kolwa oshkor**	'Eat and be Thankful' – little cake with layered pastry, nuts and syrup
بقلاوة	**baqlaawah**	fine layered pastry and nuts in syrup
زلابية	**zalaabeeyah**	fritters coated in syrup
فروت سلاط	**froot salaaT**	fruit salad
عسل النحل	**Asal an-naHl**	honey
آيس كريم	**aays kreem**	ice cream

صرة الست	**s**o**rat as-s**e**tt**	'Lady's Navel' – type of doughnut with syrup
بلوظة	**bal**oo**zah**	milk pudding
أم علي	**omm** A**lee**	'Mother of Ali' – pudding with raisins and milk
كنافة	**kon**aa**fah**	pastry with nuts and syrup
رز بلبن	**rozz be-l**a**ban**	rice pudding
بسيمة	**bas**ee**mah**	semolina and coconut pudding
بسبوسة	**basb**oo**sah**	semolina cake with syrup
معمول	**ma**A**m**oo**l**	small stuffed cake
قشطة	**qesh**T**ah**	thick cream
ملبن	**m**a**lban**	Turkish Delight

DRINKS

سفن أب	**s**e**ven-up**	7-up
بيرة	**b**ee**rah**	beer
بيرة معلبة	**b**ee**rah** **mo**A**llabah**	canned beer
قهوة كابتشينو	**qahwah** **kaapetsh**ee**no**	cappuccino
عصير جزر	A**s**ee**r jazar**	carrot juice
شكولاتة	**shokool**aa**tah**	chocolate

72

كوكاكولا	c<u>o</u>ca c<u>o</u>la	coca cola
قهوة	q<u>a</u>hwah	coffee
قهوة بحليب	q<u>a</u>hwah be-Hal<u>ee</u>b	coffee with milk
قهوة بدون سكر	q<u>a</u>hwah be-d<u>oo</u>n s<u>o</u>kkar	coffee without sugar
قهوة أكسبرسو	q<u>a</u>hwah ekspr<u>e</u>sso	espresso coffee
جن	jenn	gin
عصير عنب	AS<u>ee</u>r A<u>e</u>nab	grape juice
بيرة ستلا	b<u>ee</u>rah st<u>e</u>lla	lager
عصير ليمون	AS<u>ee</u>r laym<u>oo</u>n	lemon juice
شاي بليمون	sh<u>aa</u>y be-laym<u>oo</u>n	lemon tea
ملكشيك	m<u>e</u>lkshayk	milkshake
مياه معدنية	miy<u>aa</u>h maAdan<u>ee</u>yah	mineral water
نعناع	neAn<u>a</u>A	mint
عصير برتقال	AS<u>ee</u>r bortog<u>aa</u>l	orange juice
بيبسي كولا	p<u>e</u>psi c<u>o</u>la	pepsi cola
صودا	s<u>oo</u>da	soda water
شاي	sh<u>aa</u>y	tea
شاي بحليب	sh<u>aa</u>y be-Hal<u>ee</u>b	tea with milk
شاي بدون سكر	sh<u>aa</u>y be-d<u>oo</u>n s<u>o</u>kkar	tea without sugar
تونيك	t<u>oo</u>neek	tonic water

قهوة تركي	**qahwah torkee**	Turkish coffee
ماء	**maa'**	water
ويسكي	**weeskee**	whisky
نبيذ	**nabeez**	wine

BASIC FOODS

زبدة	**zebdah**	butter
قهوة	**qahwah**	coffee
دقيق	**daqeeq**	flour
أعشاب	**aAshaab**	herbs
مربى	**merabba**	jam
مرجرين	**marjereen**	margarine
حليب	**Haleeb**	milk
مستردة	**mastardah**	mustard
زيت	**zayt**	oil
فلفل أسود	**felfel aswad**	pepper
ملح	**melH**	salt
سكر	**sokkar**	sugar
شاي	**shaay**	tea
خل	**khall**	vinegar
ماء	**maa'**	water
زبادي	**zabaadee**	yoghurt

TYPES OF BREAD etc

سميط	**semeeT**	bagels
خبز	**khobz**	bread
خبز بلدي	**khobz baladee**	large thin flat brown bread
سندوتش	**sandwetsh**	sandwich
فينو	**feenoo**	white bread rolls
خبز شامي	**khobz shaamee**	white pitta bread

CULINARY METHODS OF PREPARATION

في الفرن	**feel-forn**	baked
مشوي على الفحم	**mashwee Ala al-faHm**	barbecued
مسلوق	**maslooq**	boiled
مقلي	**maqlee**	fried
مشوي	**mashwee**	grilled
في الفرن	**feel-forn**	roasted
متبل	**metabbel**	spiced
مسبك	**mesabbek**	stewed
محشي	**maHshee**	stuffed

75

SHOPPING

The sheer size and variety of the Arab world, some nineteen diverse countries, precludes anything here other than general statements about shopping. In broad terms, however, the great majority of shops of any size, department stores and government offices are closed all day on Fridays, which is the Muslim day of rest when Muslims go to worship in the mosques. The exceptions are barbers and hairdressers who are open for custom on Fridays, when people can get to them easily, but stay closed on Mondays instead.

Shops and offices are open on other days from about 10 am to 1 pm when they close for siesta, reopening at around 4 pm and finally closing at 7 pm. In this way poeple do not have to work in the often suffocating heat of the afternoon.

The tourist and businessman alike are usually drawn not to department stores but to the Arab bazaar, sook or casbah; it is given a different name in every city. This is usually to be found in the oldest part of the city and has often kept much the same form as it has had for centuries, with narrow winding streets and alleyways lined with many little shops and stalls. If you are a romantic at heart then this the place for you – where the Tales from the Thousand and One Nights come to life.

One thing which can be quite disconcerting for the Western visitor to the bazaar is the age-old custom of bargaining for goods, especially ornamental and artistic wares. Larger shops display prices for the goods just as in the West. Many people are timid about entering a shop to enquire the prices of goods in the bazaar but the simple rule is this: when the salesman gives a price, offer him half what he is asking and wait for his reaction. Accompany this low bid with the words 'yeftah allah' – this will avoid any offence being taken. He may well then offer the goods at a different price and you could well halve the difference again and, in all probability, walk off with the goods at a sensible price. Naturally, every case should be treated on its merits and you should also bear in mind what you consider a fair price regardless of what terms are being offered.

Apart from thousands of different types of chess-boards, samovars, and rugs the best value to be had, in real terms, is from the gold and silversmiths. Precious metals are sold by weight, not design, and there are some real bargains to be had in this area. Obviously this is one field where the scope for haggling is circumscribed but, compared to the West, prices are very favourable anyway.

USEFUL WORDS AND PHRASES

audio equipment	moAedaat Sawteeyah
baker	khabbaaz
boutique	booteek
butcher	jazzaar
bookshop	maktabah
to buy	yashtaree
cake shop	Halawaanee
cheap	rakheeS
chemist	Saydaleeyah
department store	dokkaan kabeer
fashion	azaa'
fishmonger	baa'eA as-samak
florist	dokaan zohoor
goldsmith	Saa'egh
grocer	baqaal
ironmonger	taajer Hadaa'ed
ladies' wear	malaabes nesaa'
menswear	malaabes rejaal
newsagent	dokkaan jaraa'ed wa SoHof
receipt	wasl
record and cassette shop	dokkaan esTewaanaat wa ashreTat tasjeel
rug	sejaadah
sale	ookazeeyoon
samovar	samaawar
shoe shop	dokkaan aHzeeyah
shop	dokkaan
silversmith	Saa'egh al-feDDah

SHOPPING

to go shopping	yatasawwaq
souvenir shop	dokkaan al-hadaaya at-tezkaareeyah
special offer	ArD khaas
to spend	yaSrof
stationer	dokkaan al-adawaat al-maktabeeyah
supermarket	soopermaarket
tailor	khayaaT
till	khazeenah
toyshop	dokkaan leAb aTfaal
travel agent	maktab safareeyaat

I'd like ...
oreed ...

Do you have ...?
hal Andak ...?

How much is this?
be-kam haza?

That's too much
haza ghaalee jeddan

I'll give you ...
be-aATeek ...

That's my best offer
haza aHsan seAr

Two for ...
ethnayn be ...

OK, I'll take it
zayn, be-ashtareeha

Where is the ... department?
wayn qesm al-...?

Do you have any more of these?
hal Andak al-mazeed men haadool?

I'd like to change this please
oreed oghayyer haza law samaHt

Have you anything cheaper?
hal Andak ay shay' arkhaS?

Have you anything larger?
hal Andak ay shay' akbar?

Have you anything smaller?
hal Andak ay shay' aSghar?

Does it come in other colours?
Andak alwaan thaaneeyah?

Could you wrap it for me?
momken taleffha law samaHt?

Can I have a receipt?
momken waSl law samaHt?

Can I have a bag please?
momken kees law samaHt?

Can I try it/them on?
momken ojarrebha?

Where do I pay?
wayn adfaA?

79

Can I have a refund?
momken orajeA haza wa astared qeemat-ho?

I'm just looking
ana be-aakhoz fekrah faqaT

I'll come back later
ana be-arjaA baAdayn

THINGS YOU'LL SEE

مخبز	**makhbaz**	bakery
صفقة	**safqah**	bargain
بزار	**bazaar**	bazaar
مكتبة	**maktabah**	bookshop
جزار	**jazzaar**	butcher
دكان حلواني	**dokkaan Halawaanee**	cake shop
قصبة	**qaSbah**	casbah
رخيص	**rakhees**	cheap
قسم	**qesm**	department
دكان كبير	**dokkaan kabeer**	department store
أزياء	**azyaa'**	fashion
زهور	**zohoor**	flowers
بقالة	**beqaalah**	groceries
دكان أيس كريم	**dokkaan ays kreem**	ice cream shop

→

مواد لتنظيف المنزل	mawaad le-tanzeef al-manzel	household cleaning materials
ملابس نساء	malaabes nesaa'	ladies' clothing
قسم السيدات	qesm as-sayedaat	ladies' department
الطابق الأرضي	aT-Taabeq al-arDee	lower floor
سوق	sooq	market, bazar
ملابس رجال	malaabes rejaal	menswear
مخفض	mokhaffaD	reduced
إيجار	eejaar	rental
إخدم نفسك	ekhdem nafsak	self-service
دكان أحذية	dokkaan aHzeeyah	shoe shop
عرض خاص	ArD khaas	special offer
أوكازيون الصيف	ookazeeyoon as-Sayf	summer sale
دكان سجاير	dokkaan sajaayer	tobacconist
لعب	leAb	toys
مكتب سفريات	maktab safareeyaat	travel agent
دكان بيع الأدوات المكتبية	dokkaan bayA al-adawaat al-maktabeeyah	office supplies
الرجاء عدم اللمس	ar-rejaa' Adam al-lams	please do not touch →

الرجاء أخذ عربة/سلة	ar-rejaa' akhz Arabah/sallah	please take a trolley/basket
سعر	seAr	price
الطابق العلوي	aT-Taabeq al-Aolwee	upper floor
خضروات	khoDrawaat	vegetables
لا نستطيع إعطاء رد قيمة نقدي	laa nastaTeeA eAtaa' radd qeemah naqdee	we cannot give cash refunds

THINGS YOU'LL HEAR

ahlan wasahlan, ay khedmah?
Are you being served?

hal Andak khordah?
Have you any smaller money?

ana aasef ma Andana ay makhzoon men haza an-nawA
I'm sorry we're out of stock

haza kol ma howa Andana
This is all we have

ay khedmah thaaneeyah?
Will there be anything else?

POST OFFICE AND BANKS

In general terms post offices in the Arab world open every day (with the exception of Friday) between approximately 8.30 am and 12 noon and often open again in the late afternoon and evening between 4.30 and 7.30. Many of them close on Sunday afternoons. All are open on Saturdays.

They have these opening times in common with government offices and many shops. Post offices are mainly used for sending mail, although you can often make a local telephone call from a post office (see TELEPHONES). Since many Arab countries do not have a regular door-to-door delivery service for mail, the post office usually has a large poste restante section. If you are going to be settled in a particular place for more than a month or so you may consider opening a P.O. Box yourself.

Banks are normally open during the same hours as post offices in the morning – although some will re-open in the afternoon – and you can usually change foreign currency into local currency there, although not necessarily the other way round. Often the only place where you can change local currency into foreign convertible currency will be in a large international hotel, a large bank or at an international airport. It is a golden rule when travelling off the beaten track not to acquire any more local currency than you actually require, as you may find it impossible to re-exchange it when you leave.

Each Arab state has its own national currency and although several are called 'riyals' or 'dinars' they each have a different value, depending on the country. A list of the current value of each currency is published in the Financial Times.

Here is a list of the names of the currencies in use across the Arab world:

Algeria	Dinar
Bahrain	Dinar
Egypt	Egyptian Pound

83

POST OFFICE AND BANKS

the Emirates	Dirham
Iraq	Iraqi Dinar
Jordan	Jordanian Dinar
Kuwait	Kuwaiti Dinar
Lebanon	Lebanese Pound
Libya	Libyan Dinar
Mauritania	Ouguiya
Morocco	Dirham
North Yemen	Riyal
Oman	Omani Riyal
Qatar	Riyal
Saudi Arabia	Riyal
Somalia	Shilling
South Yemen	Dinar
Sudan	Pound
Syria	Syrian Pound
Tunisia	Dinar

USEFUL WORDS AND PHRASES

airmail	bareed jawee
bank	bank
banknotes	al-awraaq an-naqdeeyah
to change	yoHawwel
cheque	sheek
collection	taHSeel
counter	kaawnter
customs form	estemaarat al-jomrok
delivery	tasleem
deposit	Arboon
exchange rate	seAr at-taghyeer
form	estemaarah
international money order	Hewaalah maaleeyah doowaleeyah
letter	kheTaab

letter box	Sondooq boosTah
mail	bareed
money order	Hewaalah maaleeyah
package, parcel	Tard
P.O. Box	Sondooq bareed
post	boosTah
postage rates	rosoom al-bareed
postal order	Hewaalah bareedeeyah
postcard	beTaaqah bareedeeyah
postcode	ramz bareedee
poste-restante	yoHfaZ be-maktab al-bareed
postman	boosTajee
post office	maktab al-bareed
pound	jenayh
pound sterling	jenayh esterleenee
registered letter	kheTaab mosajjal
stamp	TaabeA bareed
surface mail	al-bareed al-Aadee
telegram	teleghraaf
traveller's cheque	sheek siyaaHee

How much is a letter/postcard to …?
be-kam ersaal al-kheTaab/beTaaqah bareedeeyah ela …?

I would like a stamp for a postcard to England
oreed ashtaree TaabeA le-engeltera

I want to register this letter
oreed orsel haza al-jawaab mosajjal

I want to send this parcel to …
oreed orsel haza aT-Tard ela …

Where can I post this?
wayn aDaA haza al-kheTaab le-ersaalho bel-bareed?

POST OFFICE AND BANKS

Is there any mail for me?
hal fee ay kheTaabaat lee?

I'd like to send a telegram
oreed orsel teleghraaf

This is to go airmail
erselha bel-bareed al-jawee

I'd like to change this into ...
oreed oghayyer haza ela ...

Can I cash these traveller's cheques?
momken aqboD thaman hazehe ash-sheekaat as-siyaaHeeyah?

What is the exchange rate for the pound?
ma howa seAr at-taghyeer lel-jenayh?

THINGS YOU'LL SEE

عنوان	**Aonwaan**	address
المرسل إليه	**al-morsal elayhee**	addressee
بريد جوي	**bareed jawee**	airmail
بنك	**bank**	bank
مكتب الصرافة	**maktab aS-Seraafah**	bureau de change
أوقات جمع الرسائل	**awqaat jamA ar-rasaa'el**	collection times
رسم	**rasm**	charge
مستعجل	**mestaAjel**	express →

86

بريد داخلي	**bareed daakhelee**	inland postage
خطاب	**kheTaab**	letter
صندوق بريد	**sondooq bareed**	letterbox
حوالات نقدية	**Hewaalaat naqdeeyah**	money orders
ساعات العمل	**saAat al-Amal**	opening hours
طرد	**Tard**	packet
كاونتر الطرود	**kaawnter aT-Torood**	parcels counter
رسوم البريد	**rosoom al-bareed**	postage
بريد لخارج الدولة	**bareed le-khaarej ad-dawlah**	postage abroad
الرمز البريدي	**ar-ramz al-bareedee**	post code
يحفظ بمكتب البريد	**yoHfaZ be-maktab al-bareed**	poste-restante
مكتب بريد	**maktab bareed**	post office
خطاب مسجل	**kheTaab mosajjal**	registered mail
الراسل	**ar-raasel**	sender
طابع بوسطه	**TaabeA bosTah**	stamp
طوابع	**TawaabeA**	stamps
تلغرافات	**teleghraafaat**	telegrams

TELEPHONES

The telephone service varies greatly depending where you are in the Arab world. In the wealthy states of the peninsula (Saudi Arabia, Kuwait, Bahrain, Qatar and the United Arab Emirates) the telephone service rivals anything to be found in Europe or North America, with direct dialling to many countries as well as efficient telex and fax links. To make calls abroad from other countries such as Egypt, Syria and Jordan you will need to go to a large central post office or an international hotel, where there will be a special section with an English-speaking operator. Most cafés will have a telephone suitable for making local calls. In an emergency even the most remote police station or hospital will have a telephone or radio-telephone they may let you use. In many parts of the Arab world public telephones in the street are unheard of and you will need to have a coffee in a café or a hotel as a way of getting access to a telephone – although things are beginning to change and public call-boxes are being installed in some areas.

USEFUL WORDS AND PHRASES

call	mokaalamah
to call	yataSel
code	ramz
crossed line	khoTooT telefoon moshtabekah
to dial	yodeer qorS at-telefoonee
dialling tone	Sawt elteqaat al-khaT at-telefoon
emergency	Tawaare'
enquiries	esteAlaamaat
extension	telefoon farAee
international call	mokaalamah doowaleeyah
number	raqam
operator	sentraal
pay-phone	telefoon yaAmal And edkhaal al-Aomlah

receiver	samaAah
reverse charge call	mokaalamah telefooneeyah yataHammal ash-shakhS al-maTloob moHaadathat-ho dafA nafaqat-ha
telephone	telefoon
telephone box	koshk telefoon
telephone directory	daleel at-telefoon
wrong number	nomrah ghalaT

Where is the nearest phone box?
wayn aqrab koshk telefoon?

Can I use your telephone?
momken astaAmel teleefoonak?

Do you have change for the telephone?
Andak feraaTah meshaan at-teleefoon?

Can I call abroad from here?
momken atasel bel-khaarej men hona?

How much is a call to ...?
be-kam al-mokaalamah le ...?

I would like to reverse the charges
oreed an yataHammal ash-shakhS al-maTloob moHaadathat-ho
thaman al-mokaalamah

I would like a number in ...
oreed raqam fee ...

Hello, this is ... speaking
alloo, ... yatakalam

TELEPHONES

Is that ...?
hal haza ...?

Speaking
yatakalam

I would like to speak to ...
oreed atakalam maA ...

Extension ... please
farAee raqam ... law samaHt

Please tell him ... called
law samaHt qool laho ... etaSal

Ask him to call me back please
law samaHt qool laho yaTlobnee

My number is ...
raqamee ...

Do you know where he is?
hal taAref howa wayn?

When will he be back?
emta be-yarjaA?

Could you leave him a message?
momken tatrok laho resaalah?

I'll ring back later
be-ataSel behe marrah thaaneeyah baAdayn

Sorry, wrong number
aasef, al-nomrah ghalaT

90

THINGS YOU'LL SEE

رمز	ramz	code
إطلب الرقم مباشرةً	eTlob ar-raqam mobaasharatan	direct dialling
طوارىء	Tawaare'	emergency
استعلامات	esteAlaamaat	enquiries
تصليح أعطال التليفونات	taSleeH aATaal at-telefoonaat	faults service
مكالمة دولية	mokaalamah dawleeyah	international call
رسوم دولية	rosoom dawleeyah	international charges
مكالمة محلية	mokaalamah maHaleeyah	local call
مكالمة مسافة بعيدة	mokaalamah masaafah baAeedah	long-distance call
سنترال	sentraal	operator
عاطل عن العمل	AaTel An al-Amal	out of order
هاتف	haatef	telephone
تليفون	telefoon	telephone
كشك تليفون	koshk telefoon	telephone box

REPLIES YOU MAY BE GIVEN

toHeb tokallem meen?
Who would you like to speak to?

an-nomrah ghalaT
You've got the wrong number

man yatakallam?
Who's speaking?

aloo
Hello

aysh nomratak?
What is your number?

aasef, howa moo mawjood
Sorry, he's not in

be-yarjaA as-saAh ...
He'll be back at ... o'clock

law samaHt etaSel marah thaaneeyah bokrah
Please call again tomorrow

sa-aqool laho enak etaSalt
I'll tell him you called

SPORT

Sport in the Arab world does not suffer from the problem of rain and cold which commonly plagues many sporting pursuits in Northern Europe. In fact the opposite is the case; it is often too hot to run around much anywhere near the middle of the day. It is only in very recent times that many Arab countries have given priority to the development of sporting facilities, although Egypt has a long tradition of football, golf and horse-racing.

Football is by far the most popular sport and the fortunes of major Western teams are avidly followed. Much of the huge length of coastline suitable for bathing and recreation remains undeveloped in most Arab countries – but this will surely change over the next twenty years. Gambling is frowned upon by Islam but if that is your favourite relaxation then, as a Westerner, you will probably find a table somewhere in Cairo, Alexandria, Amman or Damascus – but not in the cities of the Arabian peninsular.

Two sports which are rare in the West are widely practised in Saudi Arabia and the other peninsular states: camel-racing and falconry.

In common with many other areas of Arab life the participation of women in sporting activities is rather limited and women should have modest expectations of what will be open to them.

USEFUL WORDS AND PHRASES

athletics	al-alAab ar-riyaaDeeyah
badminton	badmentoon
ball	korrah
beach	shaaTe'
camel racing	sebaaq al-jamal
canoe	kanoo
deckchair	korsee le-shaaTe' al-baHr
diving board	manaSat ghaTs
falconry	Sayd beS-Soqoor
fishing	Sayd as-samak

flippers	zeAanef
football	korrat qadam
golf	golf
golf course	malAb golf
gymnastics	jombaaz
harpoon	romH khaas leS-Sayd
hockey	hookee
horse-racing	sebaaq al-khayl
jogging	al-jaree al-khafeef
mountaineering	tasalloq al-jebaal
oxygen bottles	anaabeeb oksoojeen
pedal boat	markeb yoHmal bed-dawaaraat
racket	maDreb
riding	rokoob al-khayl
rowing boat	markeb tajdeef
to run	yajree
sailboard	lawH shoraAee
sailing	ebHaar
sea	baHr
skin diving	sebaaHah taHt al-maa' be-esteAmaal jehaaz let-tanaffos
snorkel	shnorkel
stadium	estaad
sunshade	shamseeyah
to swim	yasbaH
swimming pool	Hammaam sebaaHah
tennis	tennes
tennis court	malAb tennes
tennis racket	maDreb tennes
underwater fishing	Sayd as-samak bel-ghawS taHt al-maa'
volleyball	korrat Taa'erah
walking	mashee
water skiing	al-enzelaaq Ala soTH al-maa'
water skis	zalaaqat miyaah
wet suit	badlah lel-ghawS taHt al-maa'
yacht	yakht

How do I get to the beach?
wayn aT-Tareeq le-shaaTe' al-baHr?

How deep is the water here?
qad aysh Aomq al-maay hona?

Is there an indoor/outdoor pool here?
hal fee Hamaam sebaaSah daakhelee/khaarejee hona?

Is it safe to swim here?
hal as-sebaaHah hona amaan?

Can I fish here?
momken aSTaad samak hona?

Do I need a licence?
hal oreed rokhSah?

I'd like to hire a sunshade
oreed asta'jer shamseeyah

How much does it cost per hour/day?
kam tatakallef kol saAh/yawm?

I would like to take water-skiing lessons
oreed aakhoz doroos taAllom al-enzelaaq Ala soTH al-maa'

Where can I hire ...?
men wayn aqdar asta'jer ...?

I want to hire a sailboard
oreed asta'jer lawH shoraAee

We'd like to see some camel-racing
noreed noshaahed sebaaq al-jamal

THINGS YOU'LL SEE

شاطىء البحر	**shaaTe' al-baHr**	beach
دراجات	**darraajaat**	bicycles
ملعب كرة قدم	**malAb korrat qadam**	football pitch
للإيجار	**lel-eejaar**	for hire
شرطة الميناء	**shorTat al-meenaa**	harbour police
ممنوع الغطس	**mamnooA al-ghaTs**	no diving
ممنوع الاستحمام	**mamnooA al-esteHmaam**	no swimming
ميناء	**meenaa'**	port
ميدان سباق	**maydaan sebaaq**	race course
منطقة مقيدة	**manTeqah moqayadah**	restricted area
مراكب شراعية	**maraakeb shoraAeeyah**	sailing boats
مركز الرياضة	**markaz ar-reyaaDah**	sports centre
إستاد	**estaad**	stadium
ملعب تنس	**malAb tennes**	tennis court
تذاكر	**tazaaker**	tickets

HEALTH

Wherever you travel in the Arab world you should ensure that you are properly insured for all health risks: accident, illness and any subsequent hospitalization. The Arab world covers an immense geographical area and includes regions where malaria is endemic – not to mention many other illnesses which are rare or not found in Europe or North America. Before you leave you should consult your doctor about any particular immunizations that are recommended for the area you are travelling to.

If you only drink bottled beverages, including water, you will avoid many potential gastric hazards. Similarly you would be foolish not to wash fruit and vegetables thoroughly or, preferably, peel them.

The general standard of medical care varies greatly from country to country; from the most modern and sophisticated facilities in a large city like Riyadh to fairly rudimentary arrangements in many rural parts. Take a good supply of any special medication you need as it may be difficult or impossible to obtain it where you are staying. If you do need to purchase drugs or medicines you should look for a pharmacy (farmaasheeyah) which is normally indicated by a large green cross on a white background. A prescription is usually unnecessary for drugs which are not dangerous and which can be bought over the counter.

If you need a doctor you'll find that they tend to be grouped together in large practices, or clinics – Ayaadah. Within these clinics there will be a range of specialist doctors as well as some general practitioners. You will be expected to pay cash and it will be up to you to reclaim the expense from your insurance company.

In general terms the Arab world is conducive to good health, being very sunny, warm and dry – in both senses of the word! It should not be forgotten that the sun in sub-tropical latitudes can be extremely dangerous, particularly to fair-skinned Europeans and North Americans, and the greatest caution should be exercised when sunbathing or working out of doors. Not for nothing do the Bedouin desert-dwellers cover themselves almost completely when they go about in the sun.

97

USEFUL WORDS AND PHRASES

accident	Haadeth
ambulance	Arabat esAaf
anaemic	faqr ad-dam
appendicitis	eltehaab az-zaa'edah ad-doodeeyah
appendix	az-zaa'edah ad-doodeeyah
aspirin	"aspirin"
asthma	raboo
backache	alam feeZ-Zahr
bandage	rebaaTah
bite *(by dog)*	ADDah
(by insect)	ladghah
bladder	mathaanah
blister	faqfooqah
blood	damm
blood donor	motabarreA bed-damm
burn	Harq
cancer	saraTaan
chemist	Saydaleeyah
chest	Sadr
chickenpox	jodayree
cholera	koolera
clinic	Ayaadah
cold	zokaam
concussion	ertejaaj
constipation	emsaak
contact lenses	Adasaat laaSeqah
corn	kaaloo
cough	soAal
cut	jarH
dentist	Tabeeb asnaan
diabetes	moSaab be-maraD as-sokkar
diarrhoea	es-haal
dizzy	daa'ekh
doctor	Tabeeb
(form of address)	doktoor

earache	wajaA al-ozon
fever	Homma
filling	Hashwo al-asnaan
first aid	esAafaat awaleeyah
flu	enflooenza
fracture	kasr
gastroenteritis	eltehaab al-meAdah
German measles	al-Hasbah al-almaaneeyah
glasses	naZaaraat
haemorrhage	nazeef damawee
hayfever	Homa al-qash
headache	SodaA
heart	qalb
heart attack	nawbah qalbeeyah
hospital	mostashfa
ill	mareeD
indigestion	Aosr haDm
injection	Hoqnah
itch	Hakkah
kidney	kolwah
lump	tawarrom feel-jesm
malaria	malaarya
measles	maraD al-HaSbah
migraine	SodaA neSfee
mumps	eltehaab al-ghoddah an-nakfeeyah
nausea	ghathayaan an-nafs
nurse *(female)*	momarreDah
operation	Amaleeyah
optician	Tabeeb Aoyoon
pain	alam
penicillin	"penicillin"
plaster *(sticky)*	blaaster
plaster of Paris	jebs
pneumonia	eltehaab re'awee
pregnant	Haamel
prescription	rooshettah
rheumatism	roomaatezm

scald	samT al-jeld
scratch	Hakkah jeldeeyah
sore throat	eHteqaan az-zawr
splinter	shaZeeyah
sprain	malkh
sting	ladagh
stomach	meAdah
temperature	Haraarah
tonsils	lewaz al-Halq
toothache	wajaA asnaan
travel sickness	erhaaq wa maraD as-safar
ulcer	qorHah
vaccination	taTAeem
to vomit	yataqaya'
whooping cough	as-soAal ad-deekee
yellow fever	Homaa Safra'

I have a pain in ...
Andee wajaA fee ...

I do not feel well
ashAor be-taAb

I feel faint
ashAor be-eghmaa'

I feel sick
oreed ataqa'

I feel dizzy
ashAor be-dawkhah

I want to go to the clinic
oreed arooH el al-Ayaadah

It hurts here
aHess be-wajaA hona

It's a sharp pain
enaho wajaA Haad

It's a dull pain
enaho wajaA maktoom

It hurts all the time
fee wajaA daa'em

It only hurts now and then
fee wajaA aHyaanan

It hurts when you touch it
aHess be-wajaA Andama almes-ha

It hurts more at night
aHess be-wajaA akthar athnaa' al-layl

It stings
wajaA laadegh

It aches
mo'lemah

I have a temperature
darajat Haraartee mortafeAah

I need a prescription for ...
oreed rooshettah le ...

I normally take ...
Aadatan aakhoz ...

I'm allergic to ...
Andee Hasaaseeyah men ...

HEALTH

Have you got anything for ...?
hal Andak ay dawaa' le ...?

Do I need a prescription for ...?
hal oreed rooshettah le ...?

I have lost a filling
saqaT Hashwo aHad asnaanee

THINGS YOU'LL SEE

عربة إسعاف	Arabat esAaf	ambulance
ضغط الدم	DaghT ad-damm	blood pressure
كشف عام	kashf Aam	check-up
عيادة	Ayaadah	clinic
طبيب أسنان	Tabeeb asnaan	dentist
طبيب	Tabeeb	doctor
دكتور	doktoor	doctor (title)
الصيدلية المداومة	as-Saydaleeyah al-modaawemah	duty chemist
طوارىء	Tawaare'	emergencies
حشو	Hashwo	filling
مركز الاسعافات الأولية	markaz al-esAfaat al-awaleeyah	first aid post
نظارات	naZZaaraat	glasses →

مستشفى	**mosta_shfaa**	hospital
حقنة	**Hoqnah**	injection
دواء	**dawaa'**	medicine
على معدة خالية	**Ala meAdah khaaleeyah**	on an empty stomach
طبيب عيون	**Tabeeb Aoyoon**	optician
روشتة	**rooshettah**	prescription
عيادة طبيب	**Aayaadat Tabeeb**	surgery
أشعة	**asheAah**	X-ray

THINGS YOU'LL HEAR

khoz ... qorS/Habbah kol marah
Take ... pills/tablets at a time

maA al-miyaah
With water

marah/maratayn/thalaath maraat yawmeeyan
Once/twice/three times a day

Andama tanaam faqaT
Only when you go to bed

Aadatan taakhoz ay nawA?
What do you normally take?

laazem yakoon maAk rooshettah le-haza ad-dawaa'
For that you need a prescription

MINI-DICTIONARY

about: about 16 Hawaalee 16
(settaash)
accelerator dawaasat al-banzeen
accident Haadethah
accommodation maskan
ache wajaA
adaptor *(electrical)* waseelah
mohaaye'ah
address Aonwaan
adhesive *(noun)* maadah laaSeqah
after baAd
after-shave kolooniya ler-rejaal
again marah okhrah
against Ded
air-conditioning mokayyef
aircraft Taa'erah
air freshener moATTer
air hostess moDeefah jaweeyah
airline khaT Tayaraan
airport maTaar
alarm clock monabbeh
alcohol koHool
Algeria al-jazaa'er
all kol, jameeA
  all the streets jameeA
  ash-shawaareA
  that's all, thanks khalaaS,
  shokran
almost taqreeban
already alaan
always daa'eman
am: I am ana
ambulance esAaf
America amreeka
American *(man)* amreekaanee
(woman) amreekaaneeyah
(adj) amreekaanee
Ancient Egypt maSr al-qadeemah
Ancient Egyptians al-qodamaa'

al-maSreeyeen
and wa
ankle kaatel
anorak baalToo qaSeer
another *(different)* aakhar
(additional) eDaafee
anti-freeze moDaad let-tajmeed
antique shop matjar al-Aadeeyaat
antiseptic moTahher
apartment shaqqah
aperitif mosh-hee
appetite shaheeyah
apple tofaaH
application form estemaarah
appointment meeAad
apricot meshmesh
are: you are anta
  we are eHna
  they are hom
arm zeraA
art fann
art gallery matHaf fonoon
artist fanaan
as: as soon as possible be-asraA
  ma yomken
ashtray menfaDat sejaa'er
asleep: he's asleep howa naa'em
aspirin aspereen
at: at the post office fee maktab
  al-bareed
  at night feel-layl
  at 3 o'clock as-saAh 3 (thalaath)
attractive jameel
aunt *(maternal)* khaalah
(paternal) Ammah
Australia ostraaliya
Australian *(man)* ostraalee
(woman) ostraaleeyah
(adj) ostraalee

Austria an-nemsa
automatic otoomaateek
away: is it far away? hal howa
   baAeed jeddan?
   go away! emshee!
awful haa'el
axe fa'aS
axle meHwar al-Ajalah

baby Tefl raDeeA
back *(not front)* khalf
   (body) Zohr
bacon laHm khanzeer
   bacon and eggs laHm khanzeer
   wa-bayD
bad radee'
Bahrain al-baHrayn
bake yakhbez
baker khabbaaz
balcony balkoonah
ball korrah
ball-point pen qalam jaaf
banana mooz
band *(musicians)* ferqah
bandage rabaaTah
bank bank
banknote waraqah naqdeeyah
bar bar
   bar of chocolate qeTAat
   shokoolaatah
barbecue mashwee Alal-faHm
barber's Halaaq
bargain Safqah
basement badroom
basin *(sink)* HawD
basket sallah
bath baanyo
   to have a bath yastaHemm
bathing hat boneeyah lel-baHr
bathroom Hamaam
battery baTaareeyah

bazaar sooq
beach shaaTee'
beans fool
beard leHyah
because Alashaan
bed sareer
bed linen melaayaat as-sareer
bedroom ghorfat an-nawm
beef laHm baqar
beer beerah
before qabl
beginner mobtadee'
behind khalf
beige bayj
Belgium beljeeka
bell jaras
belly dance raqS baladee
below asfal
belt Hezaam
beside be-jaaneb
best afDal
better aHsan
between ma bayn
bicycle daraajah
big kabeer
bikini bekeenee
bill faatoorah
bin liner beTaanat Sandooq
   al-qomaamah
bird Asfoor
birthday ayd meelaad
   happy birthday! Ayd meelaad
   saAeed!
birthday present hadeeyat Ayd
   al-meelaad
biscuit baskooweet
bite *(verb)* ADD
   (noun) ADDah
   (by insect) ladghah
bitter morr
black aswad
blackberry Awsaj shaa'eA

blanket baTaaneeyah
blind *(cannot see)* aAma
blinds setaarah
blister faqfooqah
blood damm
blouse bloozah
blue azraq
boat markab
  (smaller) qaareb
body jesm
boil *(verb)* yaghlee
bolt *(verb)* tarbasa
  (noun: on door) terbaas
bone azm
bonnet *(car)* booneet
book *(noun)* ketaab
  (verb) yaHjez
booking office maktab al-Hajz
bookshop maktabah
boot *(car)* shanTat as-sayaarah
  (footwear) Hezaa'
border Hodood
boring momell
born: I was born in ... ana
  mawlood fee ...
both kolaa
  both of them koleeyat-homa
  both of us eHna al-ethnayn
  both ... and ... ... wa ...
bottle zojaajah
bottle-opener fataaHat zojaajaat
bottom *(of sea, box etc)* qaA
bowl weAa'
box sandooq
boy walad
bra sootiyaan
bracelet sewaar
braces Hamaalaat al-banTaloon
brake *(noun)* mekbaH
  (verb) yakbaH
brandy braandee
bread khobz

breakdown *(car)* taATal
  (nervous) enhiyaar
breakfast efTaar
breathe yatanaffas
  I can't breathe ma aqdar atanaffas
bridge koobree
briefcase shanTah
British breeTaanee
brochure broocher
broken maksoor
  broken leg rejl maksoorah
brooch broosh
brother akh
brown bonnee
bruise kadmah
brush *(noun)* meknasah
  (paint) forshaah
  (verb) yaknos
bucket jardal
building benaayah
bumper madAmeeyah
burglar less
burn *(verb)* yaHreq
  (noun) Harq
bus baaS
bus station maHaTTat baaSaat
business shoghl
  it's none of your business!
  mesh shoghlak!
busy *(occupied)* mashghool
  (bar) mozdaHem
but laken
butcher jazzaar
butter zebdah
button zoraar
buy yashtaree
by: by the window be-jaaneb
  ash-shobbaak
  by Friday be-Holool yawm
  al-jomAh
  by myself be-waHdee

cabbage koronb
café maqhaa
cake kayk
calculator aalat Haasebah
call: what's it called? shoo
  esmaha?
camel jamal
camera kaamera
campsite moAskar
camshaft Amood al-kaamah
can (tin) Aolbah
  can I have ...? momken
  aakhoz ...?
Canada kanada
Canadian (man) kanadee
  (woman) kanadeeyah
  (adj) kanadee
cancer saraTaan
candle shamAah
canoe kaanoo
cap (bottle) gheTaa'
  (hat) barneeTah
car sayaarah
caravan karafaan
carburettor karboraateer
card kaart
careful Hazer
  be careful! khoz baalak!
carpet sejaadah
carriage (train) Arabah
carrot jazar
case (affair) qaDeeyah
  (container) kees
cash kaash, naqdan
  (coins) Aomlah
  to pay cash yadfaA kaash,
  yadfaA naqdan
cassette kaaseet
cassette player mosajjel
castle qaSr
cat qeTTah
catacombs saraadeeb

cathedral kaatedraa'eeyah
cauliflower qarnabeeT
cave kahf
cemetery maqbarah
centre markaz
certificate shahaadah
chair korsee
chambermaid khaademah fee
  fondoq
change (noun: money) fakkah
  (verb: clothes) yoghayyer
cheap rakhees
cheers! (health) fee SeHatak!
cheese jebnah
chemist (shop) Saydaleeyah
cheque sheek
cheque book daftar sheekaat
cherry kareez
chess shaTranj
chessboard lawHat ash-shaTranj
chest (anatomical) Sadr
chewing gum masteekah
chicken dojaaj
child Tefl
children aTfaal
china fakhaar
China as-Seen
Chinese (man) Seenee
  (woman) Seeneeyah
  (adj) Seenee
chips sheebs
chocolate shokoolaatah
  box of chocolates Aolbat
  shokoolaatah
chop (food) DelaHma
  (to cut) yaqTaA
Christian name esm
church kaneesah
cigar seejaar
cigarette seejaarah
cinema seenema
city madeenah

107

city centre wasaT al-madeenah
classical Arabic al-loghat al-Arabeeyah al-fos-Ha
classical music mooseeqa klaaseekeeyah
clean naZeef
clear *(obvious)* waaDeH
  (water) naqee
  is that clear? hal haza waadeH?
clever shaaTer
clock saAh
close *(near)* qareeb
  (stuffy) khaaneq
  (verb) yoghleq
  the shop is closed ad-dokaan moghlaq
clothes malaabes
club naadee
  (cards) sebaatee
clutch debriyaaj
coach baas
  (of train) Arabat al-qeTaar
coach station maHaTTat al-baasaat
coat baalToo
coathanger shamaAh
cockroach SarSoor
coffee qahwah
coffee pot kanakah
coin Aomlah
cold *(illness)* zokaam
  (adj) bard
  (weather) baared
collar yaaqah
collection *(stamps etc)* majmooAh
colour lawn
colour film feelm molawwan
comb *(noun)* meshT
  (verb) yamsheT
come ya'atee
  I come from ... ana men ...
  we came last week wasalna

al-osbooA al-maaDee
come here! taA hena!
compartment maqsoorah
complicated moAqad
concert Haflah mooseeqeeyah
conditioner *(hair)* monaAem lesh-shaAr
conductor *(bus)* moHassel tazaaker
  (orchestra) qaa'ed ferqah mooseeqeeyah
congratulations! mabrook!
constipation emsaak
consulate qonsoleeyah
contact lenses Adasaat laaSeqah
contraceptive maaneA lel-Haml
cook *(noun)* Tabaakh
  (verb) yaTbokh
cooking utensils awaanee aT-Tahaa
cool baared
copper naHaas
cork feleez
corkscrew bareemah
corner rokn
corridor mamarr
cosmetics mostaHDaraat let-tajmeel
cost *(verb)* yokallef
  what does it cost? aysh at-taklefah
cotton qoTn
cotton wool qoTn Tebbee
cough *(verb)* yasAl
  (noun) soAal
country *(state)* dawlah
  (not town) aryaaf
cousin *(male) (paternal)* ebn Amm
  (maternal) ebn khaal
  (female) (paternal) bent Amm
  (maternal) bent khaal
crab saraTaan al-baHr
cramp taqallos al-ADalaat
crayfish salTaAoon
cream kreem
credit card beTaaqat eAtemaad

crew Taaqem
crisps baTaaTes sheebs
crowded mozdaHem
cruise jawlah baHreeyah
crutches Aokaaz
cry *(weep)* yabkee
  (shout) yaseeH
cucumber khiyaar
cufflinks zerr kom al-qamees
cup fenjaan
cupboard doolaab
curlers meshbak le-tajAeed
  ash-shaAr
curls tajAeed wa tamweej
  ash-shaAr
curry kaaree
curtain setaarah
Customs jomrok
cut *(noun)* qaTA
  (verb) yaqTaA

dad baba
dairy *(shop)* dokaan bayA
  al-albaan
damp raTb
dance raqs
dangerous khaTar
dark mozallem
daughter ebnah
day yawm
dead mayt
deaf aTrash
dear *(person)* Azeez
  (expensive) ghaalee
deckchair korsee le-shaaTe'
  al-baHr
deep Ameeq
deliberately Amdan
dentist Tabeeb asnaan
dentures Taqam asnaan
deny yonker

deodorant mozeel raa'eHat al-Arq
department store dokaan kabeer
  zo aqsaam motanawweAh
departure raHeel
desert saHaraa'
develop *(film)* yoHammeD
diamond *(jewel)* al-maas
  (cards) ad-deenaaree
diarrhoea es-haal
diary mofakkerah
dictionary qaamoos
die yamoot
different mokhtalef
  that's different hazaak
  mokhtalef
  I'd like a different one oreed
  nawA mokhtalef
difficult saAb
dining car Arabat al-'akl
dining room ghorfat aT-TaAm
directory *(telephone)* daleel
dirty qazer
disabled Aajez
distributor *(car)* destrebyooter
dive yaghTas
diving board mansat al-ghaTs
divorced *(man)* moTallaq
  (woman) moTallaqah
do yaAmal
doctor Tabeeb
document watheeqah
dog kalb
doll Aroosah
dollar dollar
door baab
double room ghorfah be-sareer
  mozdawej
doughnut faTeerah
down asfal
drawing pin daboos rasm
dress fostaan

drink *(verb)* yashrab
  (noun) mashroob
  would you like a drink?
  toreed tashrab shay'?
drinking water maa' lesh-shorb
drive *(verb)* yasooq
driver saa'eq
driving licence rokhsat qiyaadah
drunk sakraan
dry jaaf
dry cleaner tanzeef al-malaabes
  bel-bokhaar
dummy *(for baby)* Halamah
  maTaaTeeyah ler-raDeeA
during khelaal
dustbin safeeHah al-qomaamah
duster menfaDah
duty-free moAfaa men ar-rasm
  al-jomrokee

each *(every)* kol
  twenty dinars each kol
  waaHed be-Aeshreen deenar
early mobakker
earrings Halaqah
ears ozon
east sharq
easy sahel
eat ya'kol
egg bayD
Egypt meSr
either: either of them ay
  menhoma
  either ... or ... ema ... aw ...
elastic maren
elastic band laasteek
elbow kooA
electric kahrabaa'ee
electricity kahrabaa'
else: something else shay'
  aakhar

someone else shakhs aakhar
somewhere else makaan
  aakhar
embarrassing mokhbel
embassy sefaarah
embroidery taTreez
emerald zomorrod
emergency Tawaare'
Emirates al-emaaraat
empty khaalee
end nehaayah
engaged *(couple)* makhToob
  (occupied) mashghool
engine *(motor)* moHarrek
England engeltera
English engleezee
  (language) engleezee
Englishman engleezee
Englishwoman engleezeeyah
enlargement takbeer
enough kefaayah
entertainment tasleeyah
entrance madkhal
envelope maZroof
escalator maSAd
especially makhSoos
evening masaa'
every kol
everyone kol waaHed
everything kol shay'
everywhere kol makaan
example methaal
  for example Ala sabeel al-methaal
excellent momtaaz
excess baggage wazn zaa'ed
exchange *(verb)* yoHawwel
exchange rate seAr at-taHweel
excursion nozhah
excuse me! *(to get attention)* law
  samaHt!
exit makhraj
expensive ghaalee

extension tamdeed
eye drops qaTarah lel-Aynayn
eyes Aynayn

face wajh
faint *(unclear)* baahet
  (verb) yagheeb An al-waAee
  to feel faint yashAor
  be-eghmaa'
fair *(funfair)* malaahee
  (just) **it's not fair** laysa
  haza Aadel
false teeth asnaan senaAeeyah
family Aa'elah
fan *(ventilator)* marwaHah
  (enthusiast) moAjab
fan belt sayr al-marwaHah
far baAeed
  how far is ...? qad aysh
  al-masaafah le-...?
fare ojrat as-safar
farm mazraA
farmer mozaareA
fashion al-mooDah
fast sareeA
  (noun: during Ramadan etc)
  soom
fat *(of person)* badeen
  (on meat etc) dehn
father ab
feel *(touch)* yalmes
  I feel hot ashAor be-sokhoonah
  I feel like ... ashAor be ...
  I don't feel well seHatee laysat
  Ala ma yoraam
feet qadam
ferry moAdeeyah
fever Homma
fiancé khaTeeb
fiancée khaTeebah
field Haql

fig teen
filling *(tooth)* Hashoo
film feelm
filter felter
finger osboA
fire naar
  (blaze) Hareeq
fire extinguisher Tafaayat Hareeq
fireworks alAab naareeyah
first awal
  first aid esAafaat awaleeyah
first floor aT-Taabeq al-awal
fish samak
fishing Sayd as-samak
  to go fishing yazhab le-Sayd
  as-samak
fishing rod qasabat sayd as-samak
fishmonger baa'eA as-samak
fizzy fawaar
flag Alam
flash *(camera)* flaash
flat *(level)* mosaTTaH
  (apartment) shaqqah
flavour TaAm
flea borghooth
flight reHlat Tayaraan
flip-flops shebsheb
flippers zAanef
flour daqeeq
flower zahrah
flu enflooenza
fly *(verb)* yaTeer
  (insect) zobaabah
fog Dabaab
folk music mooseeqa shaAbeeyah
food tAam
food poisoning tasammom
  ghezaa'ee
football korrat qadam
  (ball) korrah
for le
  for me lee

what for? lemaaza?
  for a week le-modat osbooA
foreigner ajnabee
forest ghaabah
fork shawkah
fortnight osbooAyn
fountain pen qalam Hebr
fourth ar-raabeA
fracture kasr
France faransa
free khaalee
  (no cost) majaanan
freezer freezer
French faransee
fridge thalaajah
friend Sadeeq
friendly laTeef
front: in front of ... amaam ...
frost saqeeA
fruit faakeha
fruit juice ASeer fawaakeh
fry yaqlee
frying pan Taasah lel-qalee
full momtale'
  I'm full ana shabAan
full board eqaamah bel-ma'kal
funnel *(for pouring)* qomA
funny moDHek
  (odd) ghareeb
furniture athaath

garage garaaj
garden Hadeeqah
garlic thoom
gear Sondooq at-teroos
gear lever naaqel Sondooq
  at-teroos
gents *(toilet)* towaaleet ler-rejaal
German almaanee
Germany alemaaniya
get *(fetch)* yajeeb

have you got ...? Andak ...?
to get the train yalHaq
  al-qetaar
get back: we get back tomorrow
  narjaA bokrah
to get something back yorajjeA
get in yadkhol
  (arrive) yasel
get out yakhroj
get up *(rise)* yaqoom
gift hadeeyah
gin jenn
girl bent
give yoATee
glad masroor
  I'm glad ana masroor
glass zojaaj
  (to drink) koob
glasses naZaraat
gloss prints TebaAh laameAh
gloves qafaazaat
glue samgh
goggles naZaraat khaasah
  le-weqaayat al-Aynayn
gold zahab
good jayyed
  good! wa howa ka-zaalek!
goodbye maA as-salaamah
government Hokoomah
granddaughter Hafeedah
grandfather jadd
grandmother jaddah
grandson Hafeed
grapes Aenab
grass Aoshb
Great Britain breeTaaniya
  al-AoZma
Greece al-yoonaan
Greek yoonaanee
green akhDar
grey ramaadee
grill shawaayah

grocer *(shop)* baqaal
ground floor aT-Taabeq al-arDee
guarantee *(noun)* Damaan
   (verb) yaDman
guard Haares
guide book daleel as-soyaaH
guitar geetaar
Gulf al-khaleej
Gulf States dowwal al-khaleej
gun *(rifle)* bondoqeeyah
   (pistol) mosaddas

hair shaAr
haircut *(for man)* Helaaqat
   ash-shaAr
   (for woman) qaSS ash-shaAr
hairdresser Halaaq
hair dryer mojaffef ash-shaAr
hair spray Telaa' yobakh
   Alash-shaAr le-tathbeet-ho
half nesf
   half an hour nesf saAh
half board nawm wa efTaar
   faqaT
ham laHm fakhz al-khanzeer
hamburger hamborger
hammer meTraqah
hand yad
hand brake faraamel
handbag shanTat yad
handkerchief mandeel
handle *(door)* meqbaD
handsome waseem
hangover khomaar
happy saAeed
harbour meenaa'
hard qaasee
   (difficult) SaAb
hard lenses Adasaat Saldeeyah
hat qobaAh
have *(own)* yamtalek

I don't have ... ma Andee ...
can I have ...? momken
   aakhoz ...?
have you got ...? Andak ...?
I have to go now laazem amshee
   alaan
hayfever al-Homma al-qasheeyah
he howa
head ra's
headache sodaA
headlights an-noor al-amaamee
hear yasmaA
hearing aid samaAt al-aSamm
heart qalb
heart attack nawbah qalbeeyah
heating tadfe'ah
heavy thaqeel
heel kaAb
hello ahlan
help *(noun)* mosaAdah
   (verb) yosaAed
   help! an-najdah!
her: it's her haza heya
   it's for her haza laha
   give it to her aATeeha laha
   (possessive) ...-ha
   her book ketaabha
   her house manzelha
   her shoes Hezaa'ha
   it's hers haza melk-ha
here hona
hieroglyphs heerooghleefee
high Aalee
highway code taAleemaat
   al-qiyaadah
hill tell
him: it's him haza howa
   it's for him haza laho
   give it to him aATeeha laho
hire yasta'jer
his ...-ho
   his book ketaabho

his house manzelho
his shoes Hezaa'ho
it's his haza melk-ho
history taareekh
hitch-hiking otostop
hobby hawaayah
Holland holanda
holiday AoTlah
honest Saadeq
honey Asal
honeymoon shahr al-Asal
horn *(car)* booq
  (animal) qarn
horrible mofzeA
hospital mostashfa
hot *(weather)* Haar
hour saAh
house manzel
how? kayf?
hungry: I'm hungry ana
  jawAan
hurry: I'm in a hurry ana
  mostaAjel
husband zawj

I ana
ice thalj
ice cream ays kreem
ice cube qeTAt thalj
ice lolly masaaSah
if eza
ignition jehaaz al-eshAal
ill mareeD
immediately fawran
impossible mostaHeel
in fee
  in English bel-engleezee
  in the hotel feel-fondoq
India al-hend
Indian *(man)* hendee
  (woman) hendeeyah

(adj) hendee
indicator mo'asher
indigestion Aosr al-haDm
infection Adwa
information maAloomaat
injection Hoqnah
injury jarH
ink Hebr
inner tube anboob daakhelee
insect Hasharah
insect repellent Taared
  lel-Hasharaat
insomnia araq
insurance ta'meen
interesting shayeq
interpret yotarjem
invitation daAwa
Iraq al-Aeraaq
Ireland erlanda
Irish erlandee
Irishman erlandee
Irishwoman erlandeeyah
iron *(metal)* Hadeed
  (for clothes) mekwah
ironmonger Hadaad
is: he is ... howa ...
  she is ... heya ...
Islam eslaam
island jazeerah
it howa, heya
  it's over there howa/hiya
  honaak
Italy eeTaalya
itch *(noun)* Hakkah jeldeeyah
  it itches yoHekk

jacket jaakeet
jam morabba
jazz mooseeqa al-jazz
jealous ghayoor
jeans jeenz

jellyfish qandeel al-baHr
jeweller taajer mojawharaat
job waZeefah
jog (verb) hazz
  to go for a jog yajree
  be-hodoo' let-tarayoD
joke noktah
Jordan al-ordon
journey reHlah
jumper bloozah men at-treeko
just: it's just arrived qad
  waSalat haza al-laHzah
  I've just one left Andee
  waaHedah baaqeeyah faqaT
  just two ethnayn faqaT

key meftaaH
kidney kolyah
kilo keelo
kilometre keelometer
kitchen maTbakh
knee rokbah
knife sakeen
knit yaHook be-'ebr at-treeko
know: I don't know laa aAref
Koran qoraan
Kuwait al-koowayt

label beTaaqah
lace dantelah
laces (of shoe) rebaaT al-Heza'
ladies (toilet) towaaleet
  les-sayedaat
lake boHayrah
lamb kharoof
lamp mesbaaH
lampshade abajoor
land (noun) arD
  (verb) yahboT
language loghah

large kabeer
last (final) akheer
  last week al-osbooA al-maaDee
  last month ash-shahr al-maaDee
  at last! akheeran!
late: it's getting late al-waqt
  mota'akher
  the bus is late al-bas mota'akher
laugh yaDHak
launderette dokaan le-ghasl
  ath-thiyaab
laundry (place) maghsal
  (dirty clothes) malaabes toreed
  al-ghasl
laxative mos-hel
lazy kaslaan
leaf waraqah
leaflet warayqah
learn yataaAllam
leather jeld
Lebanon lebnaan
left (not right) yasaar
  there's nothing left la yoojad
  shay' motabaqee
left luggage (locker) khezaanah
  lesh-shonoT
leg rejl
lemon laymoon
lemonade leemoonaadah
length Tool
lens Adasah
less aqall
lesson dars
letter kheTaab
letterbox sandooq al-bareed
lettuce khass
library maktabah
Libya leebya
licence rokhsah
life Hayaah
lift (in building) meSAd
  could you give me a lift?

115

momken towaselnee?
light *(not heavy)* khafeef
　(not dark) faateH
light meter Adaad aD-Daw'
lighter qadaaHah
lighter fuel ghaaz al-qadaaHah
like: I like you ana moAjab bek
　I like swimming ana oHebb
　as-sebaaHah
　it's like ... enaho yoshbeh ...
lime *(fruit)* laymoon maaleH
lip salve marham le-manaA
　tashaffof ash-shafaah
lipstick qalam rooj
liqueur sharaab koHoolee Holw
　al-mazaaq
list qaa'emah
litre leeter
litter qomaamah motanaatherah
little *(small)* sagheer
　it's a little big enaha kabeerah
　baAD ash-shay'
　just a little kameeyah qaleelah
　faqaT
liver kabed
lobster jambaree kabeer al-Hajm
lollipop masaaSah
long Taweel
　how long does it take? qad
　aysh tastaghreq?
lorry looree
lost property Haqaa'eb
　mafqoodah
lot: a lot kameeyah kabeerah
loud *(noise)* (Sawt) Aalee
　(colour) Sarekh
lounge Salat al-joloos
love *(noun)* Hobb
　(verb) yoHebb
lover *(man)* Asheeq
　(woman) Asheeqah
low monkhafeD

luck HaZZ
　good luck! HaZZ saAeed!
luggage Haqaa'eb
luggage rack raff al-Haqaa'eb
lunch ghadaa'

magazine majallah
mail bareed
make yosawee
make-up makiyaaj
man rajol
manager modeer
map khareeTah
　a map of Riyadh khareeTat
　ar-riyaaD
marble zokhaam
margarine marjareen
market sooq
marmalade morabba al-borto'aan
married motazawaj
mascara mekHal
mass *(church)* qodaas
mast Saaren
match *(light)* Aood kebreet
　(sport) mobaarah
material *(cloth)* qomaash
mattress martabah
Mauritania moretaaniya
maybe momken
me: it's me *(speaking)* ana
　atakallam
　it's for me enaho lee
　give it to me aATeeneeho
meal wajbah
meat laHm
mechanic meekaaneekee
medicine dawaa'
meeting ejtemaA
melon shamaam
menu qaa'emat al-aTAemah
message resaalah

midday aZ-Zohr
middle: in the middle feel-wasaT
midnight nesf al-layl
milk Haleeb
mine: it's mine haza melkee
mineral water miyaah maAdaneeyah
minute daqeeqah
mirror meraah
Miss aaneesah
mistake ghalTah
  to make a mistake yaghlaT
monastery dayr
money foloos
month shahr
monument nosob tazkaaree
moon qamar
moped motoseeklett
more akthar
morning SabaaH
  in the morning fees-SabaaH
Morocco al-maghreb
mosaic fosayfesaa'
moslem moslem
mosque jaameA
mosquito baAooDah
mother nosob
motorbike daraajah bokhaareeyah
motorboat qaareb bokhaaree
motorway Tareeq ra'eesee
mountain jebel
mouse fa'r
moustache shaareb
mouth fam
move yataHarrak
  don't move! laa tataHarrak
  (house) yoAzzel
movies as-seenema
  a movie feelm seenemaa'ee
Mr as-sayed
Mrs as-sayedah
much: not much laysa katheer

much better/slower afDal be-katheer/baTee' jeddan
muezzin mo'azzen
mug fenjaan
  a mug of coffee fenjaan qahwah
mule baghl
mum mama
museum matHaf
mushroom foTr
music mooseeqa
musical instrument adaah mooseeqeeyah
musician mooseeqaar
mussels omm al-kholool
mustard khardal
my ...-ee
  my book ketaabee
  my bag shanTatee
  my keys mafaateeHee
mythology asaaTeer al-qodamaa'

nail *(metal)* mesmaar
  (finger) aZaafer
nail file mebrad aZaafer
nail polish molamme' lel-aZaafer
name esm
nappy kafoolat aT-Tefl
narrow Dayeq
near: near the door qareeb men al-baab
  near London qareeb men London
necessary Darooree
necklace Aoqd
need *(verb)* yaHtaaj
  I need ... aHtaaj ...
  there's no need laa daAee
needle 'ebrah
negative *(photo)* Soorah fotooghrafeeyah salbeeyah
neither: neither of them laa waaHed men homa

neither ... nor ... laa ... wa-laa ...
nephew *(brother's son)* ebn al-akh
(sister's son) ebn al-okht
never abadan
new jadeed
news akhbaar
newsagent baa'eA as-soHof
newspaper jareedah
New Zealand niyoo zelanda
New Zealander *(man)* niyoo zelandee
(woman) niyoo zelandeeyah
next al-qaadem
next week al-'osbooA al-qaadem
next month ash-shahr al-qaadem
nice jameel
niece *(brother's daughter)* bent al-akh
(sister's daughter) bent al-okht
night layl
nightclub naadee laylee
nightdress thowb an-nawm len-nesaa'
night porter khafeer laylee
Nile an-neel
no *(response)* laa
I have no money maa Andee foloos
there are no ... maa fee ...
noisy katheer aD-DooDaa'
north shemaal
Northern Ireland erlanda ash-shemaaleeyah
nose anf
not laa, moo
notebook daftar molaakhaZaat
nothing laa shay'
novel rewaayah
now alaan

number raqm
number plate lawHat al-arqaam
nurse *(female)* momarreDah
nut *(fruit)* bondoq
(for bolt) saamoolah

obelisk masallah
occasionally aHyaanan
octopus okhTobooT
of men
office maktab
often ghaaleban
oil *(for food, in car engine)* zayt
(crude) nafT
oil industry senaAt al-betrool
oil well be'r betrool
ointment marham
OK ookay
old *(thing)* qadeem
(person) Ajooz
olive zaytoon
Oman Aomaan
omelette oomleet
on Ala
on the ground Ala al-arD
on the table Ala aT-Taawalah
one waaHed
onion basal
only faqaT
open *(verb)* yaftaH
(adj) maftooH
opposite: opposite the hotel amaam al-fondoq
optician naZaaraatee
or aw
orange *(colour)* bortoqaalee
(fruit) bortoqaal
orange juice Aseer bortoqaal
orchestra al-oorkestra
ordinary *(normal)* Aadee

organ AoDW
  (music) al-orghon
our ...-na
  it's ours haza melkna
out: he's out howa moo mawjood
outside khaarej
over fawq
  over there honaak
overtake yatakhaTa
oyster maHaar

package Tard
packet Aolbah
  a packet of ... Aolbat ...
  pack of cards shaddat waraq
  al-laAb
padlock qofl
page SafHah
pain alam
paint *(noun)* dahaan
pair zawj
Pakistan baakestaan
Pakistani *(man)* baakestaanee
  (woman) baakestaaneeyah
  (adj) baakestaanee
pale momtaqeA
Palestine felasTeen
pancakes qoTaayef
paper waraq
paracetamol paraaseetamool
parcel Tard
pardon? Afwan?
parents waaledayn
park *(noun)* Hadeeqah
  where can I park? wayn
  awqef as-sayaarah?
party *(celebration)* Haflah
  (group) majmooAh
  (political) Hezb
passenger raakeb
passport jawaaz safar

pasta baasta
path mamsha
pavement raseef
pay yadfaA
peach khookh
peanuts fool soodaanee
pear komethra
pearl loo'loo'
peas besellah
pedestrian moshaah
peg *(clothes)* mashbak lel-ghaseel
pen qalam
pencil qalam rosaaS
pencil sharpener mebrah lel-aqlaam
penfriend Sadeeq moraaselah
peninsula shebh jazeerah
penknife meTwaah
people naas
pepper felfel
peppermints neAnaA
per: per night kol laylah
perfect kaamel
perfume AeTr
perhaps robbama
perm tamweej ash-shaAr
petrol banzeen
petrol station maHaTTat banzeen
petticoat tanoorah daakheleeyah
Pharaoh farAoon
photograph *(noun)* soorah
  (verb) yoSawwer
photographer moSawwer
phrase book ketaab TaAbeeraat
piano biyaano
pickpocket nashaal
picnic nozhah lel-akl
piece qeTah
pillow wesaadah
pilot *(of aircraft)* Tayaar
pin daboos
pine *(tree)* Sanoobar
pineapple ananaas

119

pink wardee
pipe beebah; *(waterpipe: for smoking)* ghalyoon
(for water) anboob
piston makbas
pizza beetza
place makaan
plant nabaat
plaster *(for cut)* shareeT laaSeq
plastic blaasteek
plastic bag shanTat blaasteek
plate Tabaq
platform raSeef
play *(theatre)* masraHeeyah
please law samaHt
plug *(electrical)* qaabes
(sink) sedaadah
pocket jayb
poison somm
police shorTah, boolees
policeman shorTee
police station noqTat ash-shorTah
politics siyaasah
poor faqeer
(bad quality) radee'
pop music mooseeqee gharbee
pork laHm khanzeer
port *(harbour)* meenaa'
porter *(for luggage)* shayaal
(hotel) bawaab
possible momken
post *(noun)* bareed
(verb) yorsel
post box sandooq bareed
postcard beTaaqah bareedeeyah
poster eAlaan
postman rajol bareed
post office maktab bareed
potato baTaaTes
poultry aT-Toyoor ad-daajenah
pound *(money)* jenayah

(weight) raTl
powder boodrah
prawn jambaree
(bigger) roobiyaan
prayer mat sejaadah Sagheerah leS-Salah
prescription rooshettah
pretty *(beautiful)* Zareef
(quite) ela Hadd ma
priest qasees
private khaas
problem moshkelah
what's the problem? iyah al-moshkelah?
public Aam
pull yasHab
puncture thaqb
purple arjamaanee
purse kees
push yadfaA
pushchair Arabah leT-Tefl
pyjamas beejaama
Pyramids al-ahraamaat

Qatar qaTar
quality joodah
quay raSeef al-meenaa'
question soo'aal
queue *(noun)* Saff
(verb) yaqef fee Saff
quick sareeA
quiet haadee'
quite *(fairly)* ela Hadd maa
(fully) tamaaman

radiator raadiyaater
radio raadiyo
radish fejl
railway line khaTT as-sekkah al-Hadeedeeyah

rain maTar
raincoat meATaf
raisins zabeeb
Ramadan ramaDaan
rare *(uncommon)* naader
  (steak) mashwee qaleelan
rat fa'r
razor blades shafrah
read yaqra'
reading lamp mesbaaH Sagheer
ready mostaAedd
rear lights aDwaa' khalfeeyah
receipt 'eeSaal
receptionist *(female)* mowaZZafat
  esteqbaal
  (male) mowaZZaf esteqbaal
record *(music)* 'osTowaanah
  (sporting etc) raqm qiyaasee
record player jehaaz tashgheel
  al-'osTowaanaat
record shop dukaan bayA
  al-'osTowaanaat
red aHmar
Red Sea al-baHr al-aHmar
refreshments moraTTabaat
registered letter kheTaab
  mosajjal
relative qareeb
relax yastareH
religion deeyaanah
remember yatazakker
  I don't remember laa
  atazakker
rent *(verb)* yasta'jer
reservation Hajz
rest *(remainder)* al-baaqee
  (relax) esteraaHah
restaurant maTAm
restaurant car Arabat al-maTAm
return *(come back)* yaAood
  (give back) yorajjeA
return ticket tazkarat zehaab

wa-Aoodah
rice aroz
rich ghanee
right *(correct)* SaHeeH
  (direction) yameen
ring *(to call)* yataSel bet-teleefoon
  (wedding etc) khaatem
ripe naaDej
river nahr
road shaareA
rock *(stone)* Sakhar
  (music) mooseeqa ar-rook
roll *(bread)* khobz
roof saqaf
room ghorfah
  (space) makaan
rope Habl
rose wardah
round *(circular)* daa'eree
  it's my round enaho dawree
rowing boat markab taqzeef
rubber *(eraser)* memHaah
  (material) kaootshook
rubbish zebaalah
ruby *(stone)* yaaqoot aHmar
rucksack jarabandeeyah
rug *(mat)* sejaadah Sagheerah
  (blanket) baTaaneeyah
ruins anqaaD
ruler *(for drawing)* masTarah
rum room
run *(person)* yajree
runway madraj

sad Hazeen
safe ma'moon
safety pin daboos amaan
sailing boat markab shoraAee
salad salaaTah
salami salaamee
sale *(at reduced prices)* okazyoon

salmon salamoon
salt malH
same: the same dress nafs
  al-fostaan
  the same people nafs
  al-ashkhaas
  same again please nafs
  ash-shay' law samaHt
sand raml
sandals sandal
sand dunes kothbaan ramleeyah
sandwich sandweetsh
sanitary towels Hefaaz al-HayD
sauce salsah
saucepan weAa'
Saudi Arabia as-saAodeeyah
sauna soona
sausage sojoq
say yaqool
  what did you say? shoo qolta?
  how do you say...? kayf
  taqool ...?
scarf talfeAh
  (head) mandeel ar-ra's
school madrasah
scissors maqaSS
scorpion Aqrab
Scottish eskotlandee
Scotland eskotlanda
screw masmaar molawwlab
screwdriver mafakk
sea baHr
seafood al-ma'koolaat
  al-baHreeyah
seat maqAd
seat belt Hezaam al-maqAd
second *(of time)* thaaniyah
  (in series) ath-thaanee
see yara
  I can't see laa 'ara
  I see fahemto
sell yabeeA

sellotape ® seelooteep
separate monfaSal
separate *(verb)* yofaSSel
separated *(man)* monfaSal
  (woman) monfaSalah
serious khaTeer
serviette fooTah lel-maa'edah
several kameeyah
sew yokhayyet
shampoo shaamboo
shave *(noun)* Helaaqah
  (verb) yaHleq
shaving foam raghwat Helaaqah
shawl shaal
she heya
sheet sharshaf
shell Sadafah
sherry sheree
ship safeenah
shirt qamees
shoe laces rebaaT al-Hezaa'
shoe polish warneesh aHzeeyah
shoes aHzeeyah
shop dokkaan
shopping tasawwoq
  to go shopping yatasawwaq
short qaseer
shorts banTaloon shoort
shoulder katef
shower *(bath)* dosh
  (rain) maTar
shrimp jambaree
shutter *(camera)* Haajeb al-Adasah
  (window) sheesh an-naafezah
sick *(ill)* mareeD
  I feel sick ashAor ka'enanee
  moshak Alal-ghathayaan
side *(edge)* Haafah
sidelights aDwaa' jaanebeeyah
sights: the sights of ...
  manaazer ...
silk Hareer

silver *(colour)* feDDee
  (metal) feDDah
simple baseeT
sing yoghannee
single *(one)* waaHed
  (unmarried) Aazeb
single room ghorfah be-sareer
  waaHed
sister okht
skid *(verb)* yanzaleq
skin cleanser monazzef
  lel-basharah
skirt tanoorah
sky samaa'
sleep *(noun)* nawm
  (verb) yanaam
  to go to sleep yanaam
sleeping pill Hoboob
  monawwemah
slippers shebsheb
slow baTee'
small Sagheer
smell *(noun)* raa'eHah
  (verb: transitive) yashamm
smile *(noun)* ebtesaamah
  (verb) yodakhen
smoke *(noun)* dokhaan
  (verb) yabtasem
snack wajbah khafeefah
snorkel ash-shnorkel
snow thalj
so: so good jayyed jeddan
  not so much ela Hadd maa
soaking solution *(for contact
  lenses)* maHlool le-taTheer
  al-Adasaat al-laaSeqah
socks jawaareb
soda water Sooda
soft lenses Adasaat marennah
Somalia as-Somaal
somebody shakhS maa
somehow be-Tareeqah maa

something shay' maa
sometimes aHyaanan
somewhere fee makaan maa
son ebn
song 'oghniyah
sorry! aasef!
  I'm sorry ana aasef
soup shoorbah
south janoob
South Africa janoob efreekiya
South African *(man)* janoob
  efreekee
  (woman) janoob efreekeeyah
  (adj) janoob efreekee
souvenir tezkaar
spade *(shovel)* jaaroof
  (cards) al-bastoonee
spanner meftaaH Sawaameel
spares qeTA ghiyaar
spark(ing) plug belajaat
speak yatakallam
  do you speak ...? hal
  tatakallam ...?
  I don't speak ... laa
  atakallam ...
speed sorAh
speed limit Hadd as-sorAh
speedometer Adaad as-sorAh
Sphinx aboo al-hool
spider Ankaboot
spinach sabaanekh
spoon malqaAh
sprain malakh
spring *(mechanical)* Soostah
  (season) ar-rabeeA
stadium estaad
staircase solaalem al-mabna
stairs solaalem
stamp TaabeA
stapler dabaasah
star najmah
  (film) baTal al-felm

start *(verb: intransitive)* yabtade'
station maHaTTah
statue temthaal
steak befteek
steal yasreq
  it's been stolen laqad soreqat
steering wheel Ajalat al-qiyaadah
stewardess moDeefah
sting *(noun)* ladagh
  (verb) yaldogh
  it stings *(hurts)* towajjeA
stockings jawaareb Hareemee
stomach maAedah
stomach ache a lal-maAedah
stop *(verb) (transitive)* yaqef
  (intransitive) yatawaqqaf
  (bus stop) maHaTTat baaS
  stop! qeff!
storm Aasefah
strawberry faraawlah
stream jadwal
street shaareA
string *(cord)* doobaarah
  (guitar etc) watar
student Taaleb
stupid ghabee
suburbs DawaaHee
Sudan as-soodaan
sugar sokkar
suit *(noun)* badlah
  (verb) yonaaseb
  it suits you well enaha
  yonaasebak tamaaman
suitcase shanTat safar
sun ash-shams
sunbathing Hamaam shamsee
sunburn Haraqat shams
sunglasses naZaaraat shams
sunny: it's sunny moshreq
  ash-shams
sunstroke Darabat ash-shams
suntan lafHat ash-shams

suntan lotion maHlool Dedd
  ash-shams
supermarket soopermaarket
supplement joz' 'eDaafee
sure mota'akked
  are you sure? hal anta
  mota'akked?
surname al-laqb
sweat *(noun)* Araq
  (verb) yaAreq
sweet *(not sour)* Holw
  (candy) Halwa
swimming costume malaabes
  as-sebaaHah
swimming pool Hamaam sebaaHah
swimming trunks maayoo
switch *(light etc)* meftaaH
Switzerland sweesra
synagogue maAbad al-yahood
Syria sooreeyah

table Taawalah
tablet qorS
take ya'khoz
take-off 'eqlaA
take off *(plane)* yoqleA
talcum powder boodrat talk
talk *(noun)* Hadeeth
  (verb) yataHaddath
tall Taweel
tampon tampoon
tangerine yosofee
tap Sanboor
tapestry lawHah kabeerah
  taTreezeeyah
tea shaay
tea towel menshafah le-tajfeef
  al-awaanee
telegram barqeeyah
telephone *(noun)* teleefoon
  (verb) yataSSel teleefooneeyan

telephone box koshK teleefoon
telephone call mokaalamah
teleefooneeyah
television televeziyoon
temperature Haraarah
tent khaymah
tent peg wattad al-khaymah
tent pole Amood naSb
al-khaymah
than men
thank *(verb)* yashkor
thanks shokran
thank you very much shokran
jazeelan
that: that bus hazaak al-baaS
that man hazaak ar-rajol
that woman haadeek
al-Hormah
what's that? shoo hazaak?
I think that ... aAtaqed an ...
their ...-hom
their room ghorfat-hom
their books kotobhom
it's theirs haza melkhom
them: it's for them haza lahom
give it to them aATeehom
iyaaha
then waqtzaalek
there honaak
there is/are ... fee ...
is/are there ...? hal fee ...?
thermos flask tormos
these: these things haazehe
al-ashyaa'
these are mine haazehe
al-ashyaa' melkee
they hom
thick sameek
thin rafeeA
think: I think so aAtaqed
I'll think about it sawfa
ofakker feel-mawDooA

third ath-thaaleth
thirsty: I'm thirsty ana ATshaan
this: this bus haza al-baaS
this man haza ar-rajol
this woman hazeh al-Hormah
what's this? shoo haza?
this is Mr. ... haza as-sayed ...
those: those things haazehe
al-ashyaa'
those are his haazehe al-ashyaa'
melk-ho
throat zawr
throat pastilles baasteeliya lez-zawr
through khelaal
thunderstorm Aasefah raAdeeyah
ticket tazkarah
tie *(noun)* rebaaT al-Aonoq
(verb) yarboT
tights jawrab Hareemee
time waqt
what's the time? kam as-saAh?
timetable jadwal
tin Aolbah
tin opener fataaHat Aolob
tip *(money)* baqsheesh
(end) Taraf
tired taAbaan
I feel tired ashAor be-taAeb
tissues mandeel waraq
to: to England ela engeltera
to the station ela al-maHaTTah
to the doctor ela aT-Tabeeb
toast khobz moHammaS
tobacco dokhaan
today al-yawm
together maAn
toilet towaaleet
toilet paper waraq towaaleet
tomato TamaaTem
tomato juice ASeer TamaaTem
tomorrow ghadan
tongue lesaan

tonic *(for gin etc)* tooneek
tonight haza al-masaa'
too *(also)* ayDan
  (excessive) jeddan
tooth senn
toothache wajaA asnaan
toothbrush forshat asnaan
toothpaste maAjoon asnaan
torch meSbaaH yadawee
tour jawlah
tourist saa'eH
tourist office maktab as-siyaaHah
towel fooTah
tower borj
town madeenah
town hall daar al-baladeeyah
toy loAbah
toy shop dokaan loAb
track suit badlah let-tamreenaat ar-riyaaDeeyah
tractor jaraar
tradition taqaaleed
traffic moroor
traffic jam azmat moroor
traffic lights 'eshaaraat al-moroor
trailer Arabah maqToorah
train qeTaar
translate yotarjem
transmission *(for car)* naql al-Harakah
travel agency weqaalat safareeyaat
traveller's cheque sheek siyaaHee
tray Seeneeyah
tree shajarah
trousers banTaloon
try yoHaawel
Tunisia toones
tunnel nafaq
Turkey torkeya
tweezers melqaaT

typewriter aalah kaatebah
tyre 'eTaar

umbrella shamseeyah
uncle *(paternal)* Amm
  (maternal) khaal
under taHt
underground taHt al-arD
underpants kalsoon
understand yafham
  I don't understand laa afham
underwear malaabes daakheleeyah
university jaameAh
unmarried ghayr motazawwaj
until Hatta
unusual ghayr Aadee
up fawq
  (upwards) be-'etejaah al-aAla
urgent Aajel
us: it's for us enaho lana
  give it to us aATeena iyaaha
use *(noun)* faa'edah
  (verb) yastaAmel
  it's useless ghayr mofeed
useful mofeed
usual Aadee
usually Aadatan

vacancy *(room)* khaaleeyah
vacuum cleaner maknasah kahrabaa'eeyah
vacuum flask tormos
valley waadee
valve Semaam
vanilla al-faaneela
vase vaazah
veal betello
vegetable khoDarawaat
vehicle sayaarah
very jeddan

vest qamees taHtaanee
view manZar
viewfinder moHadded al-manZar
villa feelaa
village qoryah
vinegar khall
violin kamaan
visa veeza
visit *(noun)* ziyaarah
   (verb) yazoor
visitor zaa'er
   (tourist) saa'eH
vitamin tablet Hoboob
   veetameen
vodka voodka
voice sawt

wait yantaZer
waiter jarsoon
   waiter! ya jarsoon!
waiting room ghorfat al-enteZaar
waitress jarsoonah
Wales waylz
walk *(noun: stroll)* tamashsha
   (verb) yamshee
   to go for a walk yatamashsha
walkman ® 'walkman'
wall Haa'eT
wallet maHfaZah
war Harb
wardrobe doolaab
warm daafe'
was: I was ana konto
   he was howa kaan
   she was heya kaan
   it was kaanat
washing powder masHooq
   ghaseel
washing-up liquid saa'el ghaseel
   as-SoHoon
wasp zanboor

watch *(noun)* saAh
   (verb) yoraaqeb
water miyaah
waterfall shalaal
wave *(noun)* mawjah
   (verb) yolaqqeA
we naHna
weather al-jaww
wedding zefaaf
week 'osbooA
welcome marHaban
   you're welcome *(don't mention it)* al-Afw
Welsh men waylz
were: we were konna
   you were *(sing)* konta
   (pl) kontom
   they were kaanoo
west gharb
wet raTeb
what? shoo?
wheel Ajalah
wheelchair korsee be-Ajalaat
   lel-moqAdeen
when? mata?
where? ayn?
whether emma
which? ay?
whisky weeskee
white abyaD
who? man?
why? lemaaza?
wide AreeD
wife zawjah
wind reeH
window shobbaak
windscreen lawHat az-zojaaj
   al-amaameeyah
wine nabeez
wine list qaa'emat an-nabeez
wing jenaaH
with maA

without bedoon
woman Hormah
wood khashab
wool soof
word kalemah
work *(noun)* shoghl
  (verb) yashtaghel
worry beads sobHah
worse arda'
worst al-aswa'
wrapping paper waraq
  let-taghleef
wrist meAsam
writing paper waraq lel-ketaabah
wrong khaTa'

year sanah
yellow asfar
Yemen: South Yemen al-yaman
  al-janoobee
  North Yemen al-yaman
  ash-shemaalee
yes naAm

yesterday ams
yet Hatt alaan
  not yet laysa baAd
yoghurt zabaadee
you *(pl)* antom
  (sing) anta
  this is for you hazehe lak
  it's for you haza lak
  with you maAk *(m)*, maAek *(f)*
  your *(sing)* ...-ak
  (pl) ...-kom
  your book *(sing)* ketaabak
  (pl) ketaabakom
  your shoes *(sing)* Hezaa'ek
  (pl) Hezaa'ekom
yours: is this yours? *(sing)* hal
  haza melkak?
  (pl) hal haza melk-kom?
youth hostel bayt ash-shebaab
Yugoslavia yooghoslaaveeya

zip soostah
zoo Hadeeqat al-Hayawaan

hugo

Travel Packs

Now get the tape to go with this book!

Don't go away without Hugo's audio Travel Pack in your bag!

Each wallet contains a phrase book plus C60 cassette of essential words and phrases specially designed to help you speak and understand the language without having to learn lots of grammar. Freepost this card for full details or phone 0728 746546 today . . . alternatively, enclose £4.95 and say which language you want; we'll send the cassette (with a free wallet!) by return.

Name _____ Language _____ Enclosed £ _____

Address _____

_____

_____

HUGO'S LANGUAGE BOOKS LTD
OLD STATION YARD
MARLESFORD
NR. WOODBRIDGE
SUFFOLK
IP13 0BR